International Development

International Development

Navigating Humanity's Greatest Challenge

Michael Woolcock

polity

First published in 2023 by Polity Press

Polity Press
65 Bridge Street
Cambridge CB2 1UR, UK

Polity Press
111 River Street
Hoboken, NJ 07030, USA

Eliot, T. S. (1942) "Little Gidding" in *Four Quartets*, published in *Collected Poems 1909–1962*. London: Faber and Faber, reproduced by permission of the publisher.

ISBN-13: 978-1-5095-4514-8
ISBN-13: 978-1-5095-4515-5(pb)

A catalogue record for this book is available from the British Library.

Library of Congress Control Number: 2022941532

Typeset in 10.5 on 12.5pt Sabon
by Fakenham Prepress Solutions, Fakenham, Norfolk NR21 8NL
Printed and bound in Great Britain by CPI Group (UK) Ltd, Croydon

The findings, interpretations, and conclusions expressed in this volume are entirely those of the author. They do not necessarily reflect the views of The World Bank, its Board of Executive Directors, or the governments they represent.

For further information on Polity, visit our website: politybooks.com

Contents

Prelude: An Invitation...   xi

*...to see the development process as an "epic adventure"
(Hirschman), replete with "challenge, drama, and grandeur"
(because the broad material welfare gains it can yield are costly,
their realization inherently fraught); to recognize that all of
humanity is now on such a shared journey (whether we know
it or not, like it or not); and to mindfully offer up one's skills
and resources – no matter how seemingly modest – for the
betterment of everyone, especially those who suffer the most.
We can only do what we do because others do what they do.*

1 Navigating Our Diverging, Integrated World: The Three "Developments"   1

*Whether undertaken by nation states ("national development"),
large international development organizations ("big
development"), or charities and advocacy groups ("small
development"), efforts to eliminate global poverty are the
embodiment of a quintessentially high-modern belief that
human reason and resources can transform history itself.
Achieving this requires a coherent social contract connecting
citizens and the state, and states capable of implementing
increasing complex tasks, at scale. It is national development
that fundamentally drives broad improvements in human
welfare.*

Twenty-first-century development as the leading edge of humanity's 100,000-year journey (out of Africa), made possible by an array of unique social institutions. For most of this history, however, human welfare remained low and stagnant; this changed only when levels of productivity radically improved across society, a result of unwitting initiatives to routinize material "improvement," constrain elite power, and provide universal support to society's most vulnerable members. These initiatives, launched 200 years before the Industrial Revolution, put in motion contentious transformational processes that continue to this day.

The development process increases the scale and complexity of economic, social, political, and administrative life. Succeeding at these tasks merely creates the next round of more complex challenges; failing generates cynicism, frustration, and despair. The solutions to some of these problems are known or knowable, but many – such as building the rule of law – are not; the problems need to be resolved anew by each generation, in each context. Our prevailing aid architecture was not designed to address such problems, which will only intensify in the coming decades.

For all its inherent limits and numerous flaws, the liberal international order is a modern marvel, a legacy bequeathed to us that has yielded historically unrivaled peace and shared prosperity. Even so, we need to show the same bravery, courage, and commitment of our predecessors to forge new approaches harnessing twenty-first-century technologies and sensibilities for twenty-first-century problems. Discerning how to live together, despite all our differences, remains (as it has always been) humanity's greatest challenge – and opportunity.

Epilogue: Putting Your Time, Talents, and Treasure to Work (for Others)

We live in an interdependent world; few of us grow our own food, make our own clothes, build our own houses, supply our own energy, or protect our own communities. Others do these things for us; in exchange, we offer up instead our particular skills and resources. Whether seeking a full-time career in the development business, or committing one's spare time to causes of concern, or just seeking to be more informed about global affairs, it is recognition of our deep interdependence that should inspire us to give back, to offer up, to pay forward.

Figures and Boxes

Figures

Boxes

Summary

Over the last seventy-five years, historically unprecedented gains in human welfare have been attained in most parts of the world, but the hardest challenges await, in large part because of this success. There are three distinctive ways in which development is practiced and experienced: as the activities transpiring within a sovereign nation ("national development"), as a vehicle for providing international resources and expertise at scale to these sovereign nations ("big development"), and via the efforts of charities and advocacy groups focused on the particular concerns of particular people in particular places ("small development"). Each has its place, but none on its own can address the searing policy design and (especially) implementation challenges the world now confronts – and will increasingly confront whether development itself succeeds or fails.

Consistent disappointment with efforts to "build the rule of law" over the last fifty years exemplifies these challenges and opportunities. A rare sectoral issue supported by both the global North/South and the political left/right (albeit for different reasons), such efforts have also been perhaps the "least successful" in terms of what they have actually accomplished. Persistent failure endures here because this *kind* of problem requires locally legitimate context-specific solutions, not imported "best practices" that too often change only what systems look like (and are thereby counted as a "success"), not what they can demonstrably do.

Complementary design and implementation systems are needed to address the increasingly diverse kinds of problems associated with providing basic services (order, education, health, sanitation), how to give and receive, how to engage with human diversity, and how to manage shifts in occupational demands, realignments of power (at all levels), and rising expectations. These are intense twenty-first-century versions of ancient human problems, the resolution of which requires everyone to do the hard work of listening, negotiating, compromising, integrating, and respecting. Resolving inherent contentions between different groups over what constitutes "progress," and how to attain and apprehend it, remains, as it always has been, humanity's greatest challenge.

Prelude: An Invitation...

History may be servitude,
History may be freedom. See, now they vanish,
The faces and places, with the self which,
as it could, loved them,
To become renewed, transfigured, in another pattern.
            T. S. Eliot, Little Gidding

The invention of the ship was also the invention of the shipwreck.
            Paul Virilio, Politics of the Very Worst

Most well-meaning people want to believe that their actions and charitable contributions somehow serve "to make the world a better place." At Harvard Kennedy School, where I have taught a graduate seminar for more than sixteen years, this objective is explicitly stated as its core mission. Beyond individual efforts, most well-meaning people surely also want to believe that the collective tasks undertaken or sponsored by their governments, civic groups, and favorite charities – whether in poorer countries abroad, or to redress the challenges faced by the less fortunate in their own countries and communities – are helping to "improve" lives, livelihoods, and opportunities. More broadly still, most people have some sense that the steady advance of science, law, technology, communications, human rights, medicine, transportation, and infrastructure have changed the world, mostly "for the better," and that it is desirable that these hard-won advances be made available to everyone. So understood, *development* is the process by which reason and resources are intentionally deployed, at scale, to enhance human welfare.

The abiding challenge, however, is that there may not be shared agreement on what constitutes "better," and especially how exactly any "improvement" might be brought about; indeed, forging a broadly shared and politically supportable understanding of what counts as legitimate "progress" is itself part of the development process.[1] Even where there is general agreement on what constitutes "better," it is extraordinarily difficult – logistically, politically, financially, administratively – to ensure everyone has access to clean water, safe food, comprehensive health care, insurance (of various kinds), quality education, a reliable mail service, affordable energy, and honest business practices. There is surely also broad agreement that everyone should be able to presume they will be physically safe in all places, that public infrastructure will be regularly maintained, that elections will be free and fair, that courts will uphold the rule of law, that the trains will (mostly) run on time, and that one's financial and material assets are secure – though achieving these too is a wondrous accomplishment. So wondrous, in fact, that life for most people most of the time for most of history has not been characterized by these things, even as most readers of this book can confidently take most of them for granted.

In whatever form it takes, however, the attainment of "better" is always a package deal: realizing it inexorably changes other things around it and generates new challenges of its own; if financial or medical resources are routinely squandered in the notional pursuit of improving infra-structure and public health it can lead to cynicism and despair, sometimes even outright tragedy. The development process is thus always fraught, no matter whether it succeeds or fails. Providing a formal education to everyone for at least ten years, for example, where once there was widespread illiteracy, is likely to both expand employment opportunities, promote gender equality, and enhance civic participation; but achieving this goal at scale is also likely to require providing instruction in a majority (usually national) language, thereby making it harder for minority languages and cultures to endure, while requiring minority speakers to do the additional work needed to learn new material in their second (or even third) language. Rising levels of literacy and numeracy are likely to challenge how traditional leaders secure legitimacy, to undermine prevailing dispute resolution procedures, to introduce alternative frameworks for how illness, injury, and crop failure (and misfortunes more generally) are understood, to encourage migration to higher-paying jobs, and to alter longstanding social norms pertaining to gender roles, respect for elders, adherence to religious practices, cultural rituals, and obligations to family.[2]

Similarly, expanding life expectancy by two decades (e.g., from forty-five to sixty-five years) via widespread improvements in education, nutrition, sanitation, and public health will, over time, likely be accompanied by parents having fewer children and the emergence of a new social category of people ("retirees") requiring pension systems and medical facilities for addressing their distinctive disability and disease profiles. Where once the children of large families directly supported their aging relatives, rising prosperity will mean the two or three children from the smaller family unit are likely to be geographically dispersed, their aging parents now supported by professionals in nursing homes. Where parents may once have determined their children's marriage partners, now – to their deep consternation – they may have little or no say. The same roads that promote travel and trade in goods, medicines, and services can also enable human trafficking and the spread of drugs, weapons, and diseases. We need no reminding that ubiquitous social media has both a very bright and a very dark side. Clearly, economic growth can be the basis of global poverty reduction, yet it can also result in widespread pollution and the spreading of non-biodegradable plastic to the deepest point on the planet (the bottom of the Mariana Trench), justify the destruction of irreplaceable rain forests, and entail using forms and levels of energy consumption that raise average global temperatures, thereby altering weather patterns and decreasing soil fertility, leading to mass migrations by farmers within and across national borders – all generating disruptions experienced most consequentially by those who have contributed least to the problem, and who are in the weakest position to respond.

Raising productivity – the key driver of economic growth – means entire categories of employment and ways of life are inexorably rendered obsolete. One of the most common forms of male employment in nineteenth-century England was being a wheelwright; now there are none, such skills being valiantly sustained only by weekend hobbyists. Historically, it has taken about seventy farmers to feed one hundred people, but in the wealthiest countries it now takes as little as three: in agriculture, "raising productivity" – a first-order development priority – means that, over time, sixty-seven of these seventy farmers and their families will have to find alternative sources of employment; or, most likely, will have little choice but to uproot their lives and disrupt their home communities by seeking "better opportunities" in distant cities, probably (at least initially) in informal squatter settlements. In rich countries today, a steady decline in democracy coupled with rising inequality, political polarization, and an escalation of "deaths of despair" shows that hard-won welfare gains can unravel, that material prosperity, paradoxically perhaps, creates its own wrenching social problems. The nature and scale of these challenges may vary over time and across levels of development; those challenges with technical solutions (such as eradicating polio) may seemingly be solved once and for all, but other problems (how to constrain elite power, how to resolve violent conflict, how to raise children) must keep being addressed anew by each generation, in its own way. In this latter space, "knowledge" rarely accumulates. Humans can now take color photographs of black holes 26,000 light years away by coordinating eight cameras located across the globe ... but we continue to struggle, as we always have, with how to get along with each other. "Development" makes rocket science and brain surgery possible; it also creates larger and more complex forms of ancient human problems (world wars, environmental collapse) while opening new opportunities for resolving them (multilateral forums, international law, mediation). Promoting both prosperity and security is the vexing challenge and promise of development (Bates 2021).

In the early twenty-first century, another "paradox of progress" is our apparent predisposition for taking increasingly strident either/or views on contentious policy issues, making it hard to create and protect space for finding nuanced or innovative solutions to development's vexing challenges. Viewing only the unhappy outcomes I've listed above, it is all too easy (and common) to lump them with other social outcomes one finds abhorrent in the world, and to deem them all to be the products of an insidious, all-encompassing "neoliberal" agenda promoted by corporate interests and/ or "globalists," for which the solution is the adoption of a "nation first," "post-development," or "end of development" agenda. Similarly, it is equally easy to double down on an "the end justifies the means" stance – a view long articulated to justify slavery and colonialism[3] – in which pursuing aggregate rates of economic growth excuses all manner of imposed indifference to lives, livelihoods, human rights, due process, public health, and the environment.[4] Yet economic growth is clearly the primary engine that, over the last two centuries (and especially the last seventy years), has transformed the world from one in which 80 percent of people lived in extreme poverty to one in which less than 10 percent now do (Galor 2022; Pritchett 2022). Despite today's frequent headlines of despair, the late great Hans Rosling (2018) never ceased to remind us that, in so many fundamental ways – longevity, education, health, safety – life today is vastly better for most people most of the time than it has ever been, even as much clearly remains to be done.

This complex reality of development – that it can generate historically unprecedented and widespread gains in human welfare, yet in so doing wrenchingly transform societies, the environment, and global geopolitics – is perhaps the reason why one of development's earliest and most thoughtful scholars, Albert Hirschman, referred to it as an "epic adventure" (Hirschman 1995: viii). The development process is epic because the journey is transformational yet rife with uncertainty – glorious success, tragic failure, and serendipitous muddling through are constant companions; as such it is also an adventure, Hirschman argued, infused with "challenge, drama, and grandeur." Befitting the metaphor, successfully navigating an epic adventure is more likely if one undertakes extensive preparation, has a good map and a reliable compass, seeks discerning and encompassing leadership, assembles a brave, persistent, and capable crew, upholds the golden rule when encountering strangers along the way (whether as host or guest), forges sustained commitments perceived as legitimate by all parties, and prepares contingency measures in the likely event that things don't quite go according to plan.

Alas, this is not how development is usually understood; from the outset, the dominant metaphor characterizing the development problem has been one of "gaps" needing to be quickly filled by reason and resources.[5] Here too, however, nuance is needed: there are plenty of serious problems for which careful expert assessment is precisely what is needed (e.g., deciding when to raise interest rates to curb inflation); but there are also many other key problems in development for which an imperative to provide single solutions is itself the problem (e.g., managing classroom teaching, curative health care); indeed, such solutions can be a potentially binding constraint problem blocking the attainment of broader objectives.[6] But in a world of finite resources, short attention spans, impatience with nuance, and a public imperative to show quick "results," it is always easier to prioritize the former over the latter. Development is replete with complex problems which, by definition, do not have simple solutions.

In seeking "to make the world a better place," one must therefore respect the enormity of the task and the stakes, and strive to remain humble but persistent in the face of them. If development's fated status is that of humanity's greatest challenge, then it is one for which there has never been, will never be, and never should be a single story to explain it or a simple/universal solution to resolve it;[7] the only solution is the one that we craft together at any given historical moment. Development worthy of the name thus must be a negotiated two-way process of giving and receiving,[8] not merely a matter of the experts dispensing directives, the strategists promoting their interests, the privileged showering their beneficence, or the powerful imposing their will because they can.[9] Being both good "givers" and good "receivers" is not a pious aspiration but a task requiring all parties to do the hard work of taking each other seriously, working together to help create and protect the spaces wherein the wrenching trade-offs of development can be equitably and legitimately negotiated.

As such, this short book seeks not to offer a list of proven solutions to global poverty, to promote rigorous research methods to identify them, or grand plans to ensure global peace – plenty of others have done this. Rather, it extends an invitation to "see" and regard development as being akin to an epic adventure, to recognize that all of humanity is now on such a shared journey whether we know it or not, whether we like it or not, and to mindfully offer up one's skills and resources – no matter how modest or inadequate they may seem – for the betterment of everyone, especially those who suffer the most. We are all in the same canoe, as New Zealanders like to say.

*

This book stems from a series of four ninety-minute lectures I gave on a given Saturday in London each year for over a decade (from 2008 to 2019). They were given to young lawyers working pro bono for Advocates for International Development (A4ID), an NGO connecting British lawyers with firms or organizations in the global South needing to engage legal systems in Britain or the European Union, but who lacked the resources, connections, or expertise to do so. Most of these lawyers were offering their skills as a matter of personal conviction, most possessing only passing knowledge of the broader field of international development into which they were dipping their professional toes, but who, like many others, felt a moral obligation to give back nonetheless, to offer up their particular talents as a way of helping "make the world a better place." In exchange for offering their legal expertise, A4ID's participants were offered a series of weekend seminars by various academics and legal practitioners, introducing them to various facets of law and development so that they could thereby gain a better sense of how this sub-field functioned, and thus how they might best contribute to it.

In the early years of these talks I was based at the University of Manchester, so a day trip to London to give these lectures was no big deal. (Yes, I gave all four ninety-minute lectures on one day!) But upon returning to Washington, and even when based in Malaysia for nearly two years, I felt compelled to return to London each year for this forum – not only because I wanted to honor these lawyers' efforts but because the space afforded me over the four lectures was long enough to explore issues I cared deeply about in some detail but short enough to require my framing of them to be sufficiently clear and compelling to non-specialists. I thoroughly enjoyed this experience, so upon being approached by Polity Press to prepare a manuscript on international development I decided that transforming these lectures into a book seemed an appropriate way of giving these earlier efforts a formal life, a broader reach and a longer "legacy." I leave it to readers to decide if the written (and considerably updated) form of these lectures achieves these goals.

I come to the themes expressed in this book from a rather unique standpoint, one grounded in an unusual career trajectory; as such, I have a perspective on international development that, for better or worse, does not fit neatly into the usual political, professional, or disciplinary categories. I have worked at the World Bank for the best part of a quarter century, but in the Development Research Group – so, I reside "in" the world of high-level development policy and operations but am not "of" it as such; I have too much respect for real development practitioners to ever call myself one. Within the Research Group itself, which has existed for more than four decades, I remain the first and only sociologist to have a full-time staff position among a star cast of nearly one hundred economists; from this vantage point I have written papers not only with numerous economists but also with lawyers, historians, political scientists, nurses, anthropologists, and geographers. In this realm I thus reside "in" the world of development economics but am not "of" it, either.[10] During sixteen of my years at the World Bank I have also taught part-time at Harvard Kennedy School, dating back to 2000–1. I was raised in an academic family, my instinctive approach to complex issues is to think about them in scholarly terms, and over the course of my career I have held two tenured academic appointments, but my choice has been to retain a foot "in" the academic world while not becoming fully "of" that world – mostly because I find I learn most about development (at least as it's framed, enacted, and assessed by multilateral agencies) by being more closely immersed in it, and by being surrounded by those whose understanding of what counts as a question and what counts as an answer is often rather different from my own. Others, of course, may quite reasonably and rightly make different choices, but these have been mine. That said, John Berger's (1972) adage that "a way of seeing is always a way of not seeing" applies as much to me as to anyone else, and it may well be that having a uniquely situated career path only makes my insights uniquely flawed... In any event, my hope with this book is that seasoned development professionals, scholars and students, concerned citizens, and those most directly engaged in and affected by development efforts will find these pages helpful. Better yet, I hope it may inspire its readers to do the hard work required to engage in principled ways with the vexing challenges of international development – challenges which, I contend, are only going to become increasingly important and contentious in the coming decades.

Numerous competing obligations associated with my work at the World Bank (compounded by the global Covid-19 crisis) created several long delays in producing this book. Having been granted multiple extensions, I am very grateful for the forbearance extended to me by Polity's editorial team, especially Jonathan Skerrett and Karina Jákupsdóttir. I am also indebted to reviewers of both the initial proposal and the subsequent draft manuscript for their helpful feedback, suggestions, and critique. I am indebted to Yetmwork Habte Woldegiorgies for her excellent research assistance and preparation of the key figures. I am always conscious that I can do what I do because so many others do what they do – from my family members and close colleagues to those more directly doing the giving and receiving in development. Most of my professional work is written for development researchers, policymakers, practitioners, and graduate students, but this time my focus extends to include – indeed, this book is dedicated to – all those who seek to "make the world a better place," especially those who voluntarily offer up their skills and resources for the benefit of those less fortunate, or who faithfully show up every day to do difficult work in dangerous places with vastly inadequate resources, irregular pay, little protection, and even less professional or public recognition.

I especially wish to recognize the contributions to my personal life and professional development of four extraordinary students who have taken my Harvard Kennedy School class between 2001 and 2022. First, Father Phillip (now deceased; from the Philippines); second, Mosa Rahimi (an ethnic Hazara from Afghanistan). The epic adventure of these two amazing men – raised in humble rural families in the poorest, most violent, most discriminated against, and most isolated parts of their home countries (which for Mosa included nineteen years as a refugee) – somehow unfolded in ways that led to semester-long stops in my class at Harvard. Third, Halimatou Hima (from Niger) – the first person in the history of her country to get graduate degrees from both Harvard and Cambridge, who went on to serve as the only woman on her country's delegation to the UN Security Council, and who now works tirelessly to craft hybrid education systems faithfully drawing on Niger's pre-colonial past and present to better prepare its students for the future; and fourth, Ganchimeg Ganpurev (from Mongolia), who spent much of her childhood learning the ancient traditions of her grandparents – who, after their retirement, happily chose to live as nomadic herders on the Mongolian steppes – so that, in time, she could assume the responsibility of preserving and passing along their distinctive but fast-disappearing knowledge, but who now has to choose, fatefully, between returning to Mongolia to honor that commitment or pursuing a promising high-level career at a prominent multilateral agency. Nothing I ever proclaimed in class about the virtues and disruptions of development was a mere abstraction to any of these four; they had lived it, celebrated it, and suffered painfully for it. They could also powerfully convey to others, with credibility I cannot and will never be able to summon, what the best and worst of humanity can do in the name of claiming to be "making the world a better place." Phillip, Halima, Ganchimeg, and Mosa are the quintessential embodiment of the broader message conveyed in T. S. Eliot's powerful epigraph that opens this book: all four have known both servitude and freedom, in different ways at different times; the places and faces that made them, and which they loved, have now mostly vanished, renewed and transfigured into another pattern through a combination of choices, contingencies, and events ... which in time will become another pattern, perhaps equally precarious and fraught, hopefully less so.

Even if, empirically, the heavy lifting of securing widespread peace and prosperity is shaped by larger institutional processes, political dynamics, and policy choices, this should never mean that the seemingly modest efforts of individuals and small groups don't matter. They surely do, in their own right intrinsically, and because, historically, forging moral and empathetic solidarity with others is the soil in which better policies, programmatic efforts, implementation capabilities, and welfare-enhancing priorities can grow, where greater legitimacy to a wrenching change process is forged, and justice potentially secured. It is how the epic adventure of development becomes a little less epic.

–1–

Navigating Our Diverging, Integrated World: The Three "Developments"

The following is adapted from a feature story in *The New York Times*, February 2022:[1]

Western scientists have recently discovered that a large peatlands ecosystem in rural Democratic Republic of Congo contains carbon at levels such that the equivalent of "20 years of US fossil fuel emissions" would be released if the peatland were ever to dry up. From a climate change perspective, the scientists insist that the peatlands must be protected, lest a global "carbon bomb" is detonated. But how, by whom, and on what basis will the protecting be done? Enduring tensions exist between two neighboring villages as to who is the rightful jurisdictional custodian of the peatlands, each invoking different historical "maps" and memories to make their case, while government officials preside over a deeply compromised system for granting permits to loggers. Villagers derive much of their livelihood from logging and other activities in the peatland, paid for by foreigners ... Should the villagers instead be paid to "do nothing"?

Beyond the peatland's income generating potential, villagers also maintain that it is best understood as the sacred resting place of their venerated ancestors; they have little comprehension of what "carbon" is and does, and see little reason why they should forgo lucrative income from allowing the felling of old-growth trees to address a problem – climate change – they cannot fully apprehend and to which they have contributed almost nothing, wryly noting that the journalists writing the story about them probably contributed more to climate change by travelling to DRC than all the villagers combined have done across their lifetimes. It is unclear how anyone might successfully reconcile these competing claims and interests; the tensions run deep and few sources of authority are credible in the eyes of all stakeholders. For now, it seems a lone DRC scientist has achieved broad legitimacy – based on his unique combination of linguistic, scientific, and cultural knowledge.

International development is the process by which human welfare – experienced most broadly as rising prosperity and security (Bates 2021) – is intentionally enhanced, at scale, in ways broadly perceived to be legitimate. It is humanity's greatest challenge, however, because almost every aspect of it is complex, contentious, and disruptive. Initiating an inclusive development process is hard; sustaining it is harder still; and no matter whether such efforts succeed or fail, societies and geopolitical arrangements are fundamentally altered, in the process shifting the foundations on which power, identities, status, expectations, and the formal and informal rules shaping economies, polities, societies, and public administration are structured. As the story above seeks to convey, the development process in the early twenty-first century often brings together different groups, sometimes from around the world, with very different understandings of what the key challenges are, how they should be addressed, on what basis, and who bears responsibility for them.

In the case of the peatlands in DR Congo, one group of outsiders invokes the legitimacy of science to convey their concerns about a mysterious gas contained within a unique but fragile natural resource; another group offers villagers valued jobs felling ancient trees that are part of this resource; still another group asks lots of questions, takes many photos, but struggles to even walk in this setting. Insiders, meanwhile, make contending claims to ownership on the basis of partial, dated, and indecisive documents, have little confidence that their government officials can effectively manage the situation, but agree that the natural resource in question is sacred. They are bemused that the actions of certain outsiders – indeed, their very presence – are at odds with the problem they claim to care about: outsiders have created what they claim is an existential problem, yet seem to expect the insiders, vastly poorer than them, to bear responsibility for fixing it. Only one person seems to fully appreciate how truly complex this situation is, but his unique skills – as both an insider and an outsider – cannot be readily acquired by others; indeed, his very capacity to be both an insider and outsider may render him suspect by either group.

How does "development" happen in this situation? What would "success" look like?

Needless to say, there are no single or clear answers to these questions. And that's partially the point: this might be an extreme case, but it exemplifies the kinds of vexing problems that are associated with the development process in the early twenty-first century. More precisely, they are twenty-first-century manifestations of ancient human problems. These problems are compounded today, however, because the prevailing systems for addressing development issues, and the theories on which they rest, cannot readily accommodate them. This can and must change. This book seeks to help everyday citizens, practitioners, students, and policymakers – or anyone seeking to "make the world a better place" – acquire a deeper understanding of these concerns, why they endure despite longstanding critique, why failing to address them matters, and what emerging complementary alternatives are seeking to do differently.

In this chapter, we begin by distinguishing between three different types of development. These distinctions will be called upon in each of the subsequent chapters, so it is important to be clear from the outset about what I mean when I refer to each of them. In everyday speech, these three forms of "development" – at least in English[2] – are often used interchangeably, which for most purposes is fine; but in a book exploring the different ways in which different kinds of processes and rationales are mobilized to enhance human welfare, it helps to distinguish analytically between three distinct modalities of development.

The three "developments"

Development is history in a hurry. This pithy summation, provided to me by a British academic colleague one day as we pondered the vagaries of our field, has stuck with me over the years. This is because I have come to think that, as articulated, it deftly conveys that there are in fact two primary forms of "development": the first is one that happens as a historical geopolitical process presided over (if not "guided") by national governments, with all its associated triumphs, trials, and tribulations; for convenience, let's call this "national development." It is the space wherein the vast majority of development work has taken place and continues to take place: building roads, educating students, collecting taxes, regulating firms, courting investors, managing trade. In one form or another, schools, mobile phones, health clinics, and fertilizer would still be present in today's poorest countries if no international development agencies had ever existed.

A second form of development, however, entails an array of technical experts casting their gaze upon this broad canvas of historical experience, apprehending key "lessons" from their observations, deeming the essence of them to be amenable to human reason and resources, and concluding that these lessons can (and should) be distilled into discrete projects, reforms, advice, policies, and practices that will help countries attain their national objectives, thereby helping these countries do their part in contributing to the global targets embodied in the Sustainable Development Goals (SDGs).[3] By adopting this array of operationalized and profession-alized assistance, the premise is that a nation's development objectives can be achieved more efficiently, more effectively, at a faster pace, and at a larger scale than they might otherwise have been. Upgrading public financial management systems, enhancing agricultural productivity, modernizing health facilities, promoting justice reform, financing infrastructure, expanding access to vaccines, and helping mitigate climate change are just some of the many issues addressed by multilateral organizations (World Bank, Asian Development Bank), bilateral agencies (USAID, Sida),[4] and major foundations (Gates, Ford, Open Society); for convenience, let's call all such organizations "big development."[5]

But in practice such intensive large-scale efforts are almost always messy, expensive, and contentious, so in recent decades a third form of "development" has emerged with a more targeted focus, working with particular people enduring specific challenges requiring more customized responses with more immediate and tangible "results" – by way of juxtaposition, let's call this "small development."[6] In this space, a broad array of activities are conducted by domestic charities, advocacy groups, and non-government organizations (NGOs), offering programs ranging from microcredit and job training to disaster relief and assistance for refugees. A familiar example of such activity, often emotionally promoted in magazines, is child sponsorship, in which a citizen in a rich country provides a small sum of money each month to a child from a poor household in a poor country to ensure the child's household can meet basic living expenses (food, clothing, shelter, education, health). This transaction is overseen by an agency who, for a small fee, brokers and monitors the arrangement. Rigorous evaluations suggest that providing such assistance can indeed make a positive difference in these children's lives, well into adulthood (Wydick et al. 2013). Which is great – there is plenty of scope for these types of efforts, and it's one to which everyone can and should readily contribute, no matter how seemingly modest or inadequate their offering may appear vis-à-vis the scale of the problem. Doing one's homework on "small development" organizations, and financially supporting those that one trusts, is a mutually beneficial way in which everyone can provide modest financial support to, and forge some measure of empathetic solidarity with, those in need.

That said, an abundance of "small development" programs, even relatively large ones, is not what enabled Vietnam in 1980 to become Vietnam in 2010, having undergone one of history's fastest episodes of sustained growth and widespread poverty reduction (World Bank 2016);[7] neither is it how today's prosperous countries became prosperous. If the world is serious about reducing the global rate of extreme poverty below 3 percent by 2030 – the first of the Sustainable Development Goals, ratified by 193 governments in 2015 – as well as achieving pretty much all the other sixteen goals, then the heavy lifting will be done by national development (Pritchett 2022). Both big and small development can, in their own way, be complements to and facilitators of national development: each has its own tasks, requires its own skills, operates under different mandates and revenue streams, functions and assesses its work in different ways, and draws on varying sources of legitimacy. When the respective actions of national, big, and small development are coherent, coordinated, and cooperative, amazing things can happen to enhance peace and prosperity; when they are incoherent, uncoordinated, unaccountable, and working at cross-purposes, their fruit can be enduring cynicism, frustration, and despair.

There are variants within each of these three "developments," but for present purposes such a categorization enables us to see distinctively different modes and logics of engagement. National development – the work done or overseen by the state (or for which it is responsible even if it's not the direct provider, e.g., water, education), in partnership with private firms and civil society – is the key engine, even as final outcomes are also the product of broader geopolitical engagements with neighboring states and the world more generally (through processes generally referred to as "globalization"). Finding the elusive "narrow corridor" (Acemoglu and Robinson 2019) that balances the delicate state–society tension between rights, responsibilities, and authority is the foundational context within which the epic adventure of development plays out.

The category of national development is also important because it helps us recognize the different roles that big development plays in different kinds of countries. In large states such as Brazil, India, Indonesia, and China, the combined financial contributions of international development actors, big or small, amounts to barely a rounding error in the national accounts; but large countries can absorb sums that are relatively sizeable for development agencies, meaning that big development needs these large countries vastly more than the large countries need them. Matters are rather different in the smallest poor countries, where big development may effectively be the lender of last resort, its injections of funds potentially playing a decisive role in keeping such countries solvent. But smaller poor countries are often also countries riddled with numerous challenges, raising the financial costs, transaction costs, and physical risks associated with lending or granting them money, with issues such as conflict and disease readily spilling across borders, creating regional "hot spots" (Corral et al. 2020). Making matters worse, such countries are where many of the most consequential effects of climate change are likely to be experienced – by those who contributed least to the problem but are least well placed to deal with it (World Bank 2020e). For national governments in these countries especially, and for both big and small development agencies, the stakes are highest where the specific knowledge and capability needed to confidently address the underlying issues remains elusive.

There are two primary reasons for distinguishing between these three different forms of development from the outset. First, because understanding the dynamics of the history of development prior to World War II requires a focus on national (and subnational) states, not "big or "small" international agencies as we currently understand them (because, for the most part, they did not exist). Moreover, as already noted, most of the heavy lifting in development today, especially in the largest countries, continues to be a function of activities undertaken, overseen, or shaped by nation states – what we are calling national development. And second, because the ideas, processes, actors, and political imperatives shaping development today, especially since the early 1990s, are more varied and complex; as such, it helps for analytical purposes to bracket these relatively recent factors into the two broad categories of "big development" (primarily today's multilateral and bilateral agencies) and "small development" (the activities of non-government organizations, charities, and advocacy groups).

*

Over the last 200 years, and the most recent seventy years in particular, the world has gone from an extreme poverty rate of 94 percent (in 1800) to 72 percent (in 1950) to 9.4 percent (in 2018).[8] As conveyed in the Sustainable Development Goals, the world has committed itself to reducing the global rate of extreme poverty to 3 percent by 2030, though the combined effects of Covid, conflict, and climate change now appear to mean that this mark will be missed, perhaps by five years or more. Such setbacks, however, should only be a call to redouble collective efforts, not a counsel of despair; they may delay the global goal of ending extreme poverty, but they should not be allowed to derail it.

As an empirical matter, the "letter" of the global goal can largely be realized if the eight most populous poor countries have high and sustained rates of inclusive economic growth. But the "spirit" of the goal of course requires a broader analytical focus on tracking and understanding the trajectory of *every* country's efforts to meet the material needs of its most vulnerable citizens. Importantly, trends that may be true for the world as a whole, or even for regions, do not always reflect the extent to which extreme poverty reduction is being attained (or not) in specific places or for particular groups. As Figure 1.1 indicates,[9] some poor countries (and areas within countries) eliminated extreme poverty at a very low level of development (such as Egypt, 2010,[10] which did so on a median level of income of around $1,600), while others at the same level of economic development had much higher rates of extreme poverty (such as Bolivia, 2002).[11] Levels of inequality are crucial determinants of whether median levels of economic development reduce extreme poverty. Some countries are well on track to eliminating extreme poverty, even as rates of poverty reduction in others unfortunately remain stuck, have intensified (Lebanon; Iraq between 2010 and 2020[12]), or have not yet reduced extreme poverty below 3 percent, despite having achieved relatively high median per capita consumption (such as Panama, 2014).[13] The spirit of the global goal demands finding coherent explanations for this variation and enacting a corresponding response strategy customized to the specifics of each country context.

In the sections that follow, we focus on the ways in which political dynamics and policy implementation capability shape a country's economic growth and, in turn, influence whether and how its rates of growth benefit that country's poorest members. The central message is that reducing extreme poverty rates below 3 percent is largely a matter of national development – that is, of ministries within national governments being willing and able to implement policies promoting inclusive, sustained, and sustainable economic growth to a median per capita income level of at least $1,600 (Figure 1.1). Doing so, in turn, is a product of a durable, legitimate, and inclusive social contract binding citizens, firms, and the state, and of building a public administration capable of effectively implementing increasingly complex policies – equitably, for all, at scale, in ways perceived to be locally legitimate. Economic growth, social inclusion, political accountability, and administrative capability are four mutually reinforcing elements of the development process generally, and the basis of long-run poverty reduction in particular.

Despite laudable progress overall, there remains wide variation in the extent to which governments are in fact willing and able to advance these four elements – consistently, legitimately, for everyone – because of complementary strengths and weaknesses residing in the private sector and civil society, and the constraints imposed by the global political economy (over which poor countries in particular often have little influence). Overly "strong societies" or unduly powerful firms, for example, can capture or compromise the state and use its resources and authority to serve their own particular

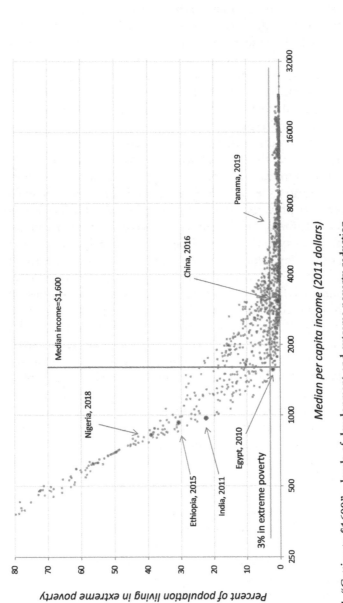

Figure 1.1 "Getting to $1600" – levels of development and extreme poverty reduction

Source: Author's calculations, from World Bank PovcalNet database, Global Database of Shared Prosperity (GDSP). All historical spells. ($1.90/day poverty rate, 161 countries, 1,439 observations)

(even predatory) interests (Migdal 1988, 2001; Acemoglu and Robinson 2019). Similarly, governments accountable only to their leaders are unlikely to be trusted by citizens or able to generate adequate fiscal revenues, especially for spending on public goods (Besley and Persson 2009). In such circumstances, the key to reform is not necessarily "less" or "more" government, as popular policy debates frequently frame it, but "better" (or "smarter") government – a responsive and accountable public sector that is informed, supported, complemented, and constrained by competitive markets, cohesive communities, an open media, and an independent judiciary, all contributing to a shared collective vision. Finding and consolidating this positive but fraught and fragile equilibrium is a defining task of the development process: there are many ways to get it right – and even more ways to get it wrong.

Four key elements of a national development process

National development gets you poverty reduction; moving targeted groups of people from one side of a "poverty line" to the other – e.g., from living on $1.80 a day to $2.00 a day – is a modest gain in human welfare for this particular group, or "small development."[14] From its founding in the aftermath of World War II, and the emergence of a host of new sovereign states in the post-colonial period, development has been widely understood as the realization of a process of societal transformation comprising four key elements (Pritchett et al. 2013). Low-income countries embarking on this journey sought – and today continue to seek – to build (a) a modern *economy based on productivity growth* (not merely the extraction of natural resources or exploitation of workers); (b) a *polity wherein key decisions reflect the aggregate preferences of citizens*, grounded in and legitimized by a mutual relationship of rights, responsibilities, and obligations between citizens and the state (not the arbitrary rule of autonomous elites, and the one-way extraction of rents from subjects); (c) a *society characterized by social equality*[15] and a shared sense of national purpose, pride, and belonging (not a society riven by overt hierarchy, exclusion of certain groups, and low collective identity); with all aspects underpinned by (d) a professional system of *public administration based on principles of merit, independence, and service* (not patronage, elite capture, and personal enrichment) capable of implementing policy. For present purposes, the nature and extent of relations between these four elements comprise a society's "social contract"[16] (see below).

In recent decades the world has made reasonably good progress on the first aspect – building a modern economy – as measured by sustained rates of inclusive growth, despite financial crises and widening inequalities. There remains considerable variation in the extent to which countries can generate stable rates of growth over long periods of time, especially in Africa, and even with similar rates of growth in rich and poor countries the absolute economic gaps between them will likely continue to grow ("big time"; Pritchett 1997). Even so, at least until early 2020, the world's economic prospects had been steadily improving for some twenty-five years (World Bank 2020c). Indicators of political legitimacy, freedom, and rights in most countries also showed steady improvement from the mid-1990s to the mid-2000s, though Freedom House (2020) reports that since 2005 there have been fourteen consecutive years of steady decline in "global freedom," with "individuals in 64 countries experience[ing] deterioration in their political rights and civil liberties while those in just 37 experience[ing] improvements ... More than half of the countries that were rated Free or Not Free in 2009 have suffered a net decline in the past decade." This decline has been associated with the rise of authoritarian governments in several large countries (even if such governments themselves were democratically elected).[17] Social equality measures – such as the rising approval for and practice of inter-racial (inter-ethnic and inter-caste) marriage, steadily increasing gender equality, and increasingly favorable attitudes to social diversity, especially among the young – have also moved in a mostly positive direction (albeit vastly too slowly on some measures, e.g., the incidence of gender-based violence; enduring racism) while sometimes eliciting violent responses.[18] But as Saraki (2016) concludes, surveying an array of recent evidence, "while the status quo is unacceptable, the longer-term trend is pointed towards gender equality. And this trend is global, not simply confined to the western world."

Comparatively, however, there remains a consistent and widespread decline in the fourth domain: quality of public administration, as measured by global data on "government effectiveness," or the extent to which states are able to implement their policy commitments. Comprehensive country-level governance data has been collected since the mid-1990s, and while certain component aspects are generally improving – "control of corruption," for example[19] – the picture is much less happy on the broader question of whether governments can do their more routine everyday work: oversee education and health programs, build and maintain infrastructure, protect lives and property. As Figure 1.2 shows, since the mid-1990s, on average, the administrative capability

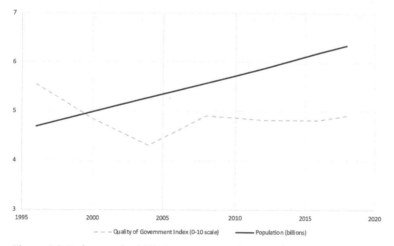

Figure 1.2 In low- and middle-income countries, populations are rising but government quality is falling

Source: Author's extension of Pritchett (2020b) using World Bank population data and country classifications. Links to the data and methodology used to calculate state capability measures and trends (using various approaches, which broadly yield consistent outcomes) are available within Pritchett (2020b)

of governments in developing countries has been steadily declining, not improving, even as the policy challenges they confront have become more complex and their popula- tions ever larger. In addition to having even more citizens needing key services in the coming years – many African countries are projected to double their populations by 2050 – these trends mean that "developing countries are dealing with a world with greater and greater complexity, more inter-connectedness – and new and unexpected shocks like COVID-19 – all with the same, or less, capability as more than two decades ago" (Pritchett 2020b).[20]

If this downward trend is true on average, it is also the case that there is considerable variation around it – some developing countries have indeed improved their quality of government (or certain aspects of it), even as many have stayed the same and others have declined. Figure 1.3 arrays this variation, revealing the disconcerting reality that state capability for policy implementation in most developing countries is stagnant or declining. An implication of this is that it will take a country like Guatemala, at its current pace (i.e., very slow improvement), several *centuries* to reach the level of today's least-capable OECD countries (Andrews et al. 2017: 23). And logically, of course, countries in consistent decline will never get there.

These diverging trends over the last quarter century in the four key elements of the development process – improving economic growth; modest but highly variable gains in political accountability and social equality; declining quality of public administration – requires some explaining. How can life be mostly getting better for most people economically, socially, and politically, while the quality of their public institutions steadily erodes? A comprehensive response is beyond the scope of this book, but there are two likely answers. The first is that improvements in technical policies – "stroke-of- the-pen" reforms such as better macroeconomic policy, the passing/removal of regulations – and widespread shifts in social norms have improved outcomes without requiring, for the moment, corresponding improvements in the day-to-day implementation work of public administration. When one

Trend, 1996–2018		Total by level of capability	Collapsing (g<−.05)	Slow negative (−.05<g<0)	Slow positive (0<g<.05)	Rapid positive (g>.05)	Percent of all developing countries
Strong capability (l>6.5)	Countries			CHL	URY, KOR, SGP	ARE, HKG	
	Number	6	0	1	3	2	5.4%
Moderate capability (4<l<6.5)	Countries		TTO, KWT, ZAF, PRI	PER, LSO, BRA, PHL, MNG, PAN, MAR, LKA, SEN, ARG, TUN, THA, IND, BHR, NAM, OMN, CRI, BWA	BFA, SWZ, COL, TUR, ARM, VNM, CUB, GHA, CHN, JAM, JOR, SAU, MUS, MYS	KAZ, IDN, RWA, GEO, QAT	
	Number	41	4	18	14	5	36.9%
Weak (2.5<l<4)	Countries		MDG, LBN, MRT	GIN, NIC, MOZ, GTM, KGZ, MLI, GAB, TGO, PNG, IRN, PAK, BOL, NPL, UGA, MWI, TZA, MEX, BEN, EGY, DOM, GMB	AGO, KHM, CMR, NGA, UZB, MMR, LAO, SLE, BGD, HND, PRY, NER, SLV, DZA, KEN, CIV, ZMB, ETH, ECU	LBR, AZE	
	Number	45	3	21	19	2	40.5%
Fragile (l<2.5)	Countries		YEM, VEN, SYR, LBY, ERI, ZWE	SOM, PRK, CAF, BDI, GNB, TCD, HTI, SDN, TKM	AFG, IRQ, TJK, COG		
	Number	19	6	9	4	0	17.1%
Total by rate of change			13	49	40	9	
Percent by growth category			11.7%	44.1%	36.0%	8.1%	100% (111 total)

Figure 1.3 Changes in state capability, 1996–2018

Source: Adapted from Pritchett 2020a, updating Pritchett et al. (2017: 20) with data from the Worldwide Governance Indicators (WGI), 1996–2018. "State Capability" is the simple average of three WGI Indicators – Rule of Law, Government Effectiveness, and Control of Corruption, on a zero (lowest country ever) to ten (highest country ever) scale

examines those aspects of policy and programs whose efficacy requires significant ongoing non-technical (or "adaptive") problem-solving, such as classroom teaching, the implementation failures become readily apparent (World Bank 2018b).[21] Similarly, if previously it was the case that many poor people received essentially no public services at all (e.g., education, sanitation) but now receive something, significant welfare improvements can be gained even if the quality of those services is low (e.g., no school in the past, but now at least a bad one), especially if the metric used to assess effectiveness is merely the provision of inputs rather than outcomes (e.g., school attendance rather than the more vexing task of improving learning). But neither aspect is sustainable – there is surely only so much gain that can be secured from technical reforms alone and the initial provision of (poor quality) services. As policy problems become increasingly complex in the coming years, and as citizens' expectations for improved quality of services inexorably increases, effective responses will rely heavily on implementation systems capable of handling non-technical ("adaptive") challenges, at scale.

The second possible answer is that a combination of vibrant social networks and the widespread uptake of low-cost digital technology can generate economic growth for a while, stitched together and "managed" by a labyrinth of informal "deals" (Pritchett et al. 2018). But such growth is decidedly vulnerable to shocks of various kinds and is ultimately constrained in size by the inherently limited reach of prevailing social networks. Modern economic growth requires a transition at some point from a political anthropology of idiosyncratic "deals" to a political economy mediated by formal, impartial "rules" ultimately mediated and upheld by legal professionals. Trying to "do development," however, by funding public administration reform projects that amount to external experts overlaying a thin veneer of visible "best-practice" "rules" on top of thick, anthropological layers of non-legible "deals" is the essence of institutional isomorphism – i.e., creating a system that *looks* modern (and can be scored as such, thereby securing a measure of external legitimacy and continued funding) rather than actually performing like one (Andrews 2013). Such an approach is fated to eventual collapse once it confronts challenges (such as a major public health or financial crisis) it manifestly cannot handle. In both the private and public sectors, a key development challenge is thus to incrementally reduce the gap between de jure and de facto rules systems – that is, between the formal rules/laws "on the books" and the informal rules/deals as actually practiced (Hallward-Driemeier and Pritchett 2015).[22]

The broader and more important question is why the public sector's implementation capability seems to have stagnated or declined in so many developing countries in the last two decades, despite the billions spent on "capacity building" initiatives and the clear importance of providing basic services and public goods to enhance human well-being. One answer is that the scale and complexity of the tasks the public sector is expected to deliver in the twenty-first century (e.g., education for all), along with the expectations of citizens, have simply increased much faster than the financial resources and administrative capabilities of the systems charged with delivering them. A related point is that much of the discussion in development debates centers on the merits of adopting particular "policies" – i.e., discussing what governments *should* do, given the problems they've identified – but relatively little attention is given to assessing the designated agency's corresponding implementation capability, i.e., the extent to which governments *can* do what they aspire to achieve and, if they cannot, how they might reasonably acquire the necessary level of organizational capability (and financial resourcing) to do so. If any policy is only as good as its implementation, then identifying the optimal policy is a necessary but deeply insufficient step to realizing the policy's goals.

Another possible answer is that the orthodox strategies deployed to build capacity – training courses, technology upgrades, transfer of best practices – have mostly changed what systems look like but not what they can actually do (Andrews et al. 2017). While such approaches may be appropriate for improving technical aspects of a reform process, they are less well suited to engaging with non-technical aspects inherently requiring extensive face-to-face interaction and discretionary judgment (Pritchett and Woolcock 2004; Honig 2018). To the extent that such non-technical aspects comprise an increasingly large proportion of the problems of twenty-first-century public administration, and failure to address them in turn becomes the "binding constraint" on effective implementation, doubling down on traditional approaches to public sector reform will itself become part of the problem of, not the solution to, declining state capability.

The implementation capability of a country's public administration is shaped not only by the skills, experience, and morale of its staff but also by the broader political economy arrangements in which it is embedded. Such factors shape the amount of funding it receives, the social status it is accorded, the types of policies it is asked to implement (or not), the level of independence its professional decisions are granted from political imperatives (e.g., to raise/lower interest rates), whether and how its actions are assessed, and the broader level of social trust it can call upon. (This is especially important when its actions impose unwanted obligations, such as raising taxes, regulating firms, imposing order, or requiring "social distancing.") The analytical space within which these political economy dynamics take place is often referred to as the "social contract": it is where and how the state, civil society, and firms – the three major sources of power – engage one another. The nature and extent of a country's social contract is a defining driver of the development process generally ("getting to $1,600") and of poverty reduction in particular (ensuring national wealth benefits the bottom 40 percent of the distribution).

Why the "social contract" matters: balancing the power of states, societies, and firms

In both legal and informal ways, a functioning social contract underpins the central tasks of society: collecting revenue and spending it on public goods (Besley 2020); regulating firms (including banks) so that competition between them is more open and equitable (Barth et al. 2012); enabling contracts to be established between strangers so that complex economic exchange can be readily conducted (Pistor 2019); sustaining respectful social interaction, norms of reciprocity, and broad-based trust so that most everyday transactions occur smoothly and at low cost, enabling problems to be solved amicably and promptly across time, space, and groups (Fukuyama 1995; Rajan 2019).[23] Where states, firms, and societies act as forms of countervailing power to curb each other's excesses, and act as complements to each other's strengths while complementing their respective weaknesses, a robust social contract becomes the foundation on which sustained and inclusive economic growth is established and thus by which poverty steadily declines. Such is the precarious nature of the path to this space, however, that it has recently been called "the narrow corridor" (Acemoglu and Robinson 2019).

Alas, attaining this functional balance often proves elusive, with the poorest citizens paying the highest price, especially when basic services and civic order cannot be provided. The poor are least well placed to deal with the consequences of a fragile or broken social contract – ill-health, malnutrition, insecurity, injustice, violence, unemployment (Krishna 2011) – while lacking the financial resources to pay for private alternatives. The rich, for example, can employ security guards to protect their property, or can send their children to private schools and hospitals if the public ones are inadequate. It is very hard to establish and maintain a functioning social contract; in the grand scheme of human history, it is only quite recently that any such productive balance between states, firms, and societies has been attained and sustained anywhere (even in Europe; see Box 1.1), yet the entire development enterprise rests on the premise that it can and should be achieved everywhere, relatively quickly.

Even in wealthy countries such as the United States, however, the social contract can become frayed, with dire consequences for the poor. In the US in January 2020, over 580,000 people were homeless;[25] in recent years, suicides from opioid overdoses – "deaths of despair" (Case and

Box 1.1 Redressing inequality in Europe and Central Asia: state capability and the social contract

A recent World Bank report on the social contract in Europe and Central Asia (Bussolo et al. 2019) stresses the importance of redistribution and taxation for both reducing inequality and broadly enhancing the welfare of citizens. In this region, perhaps as a legacy of the Soviet era, citizens are often supportive in principle of policies to reduce inequality, though in practice this means taxing wealthier citizens and redistributing the gains to society's less fortunate members, which at an individual level may not always be popular among those with the greatest political influence (i.e., the wealthy). A vibrant social contract, however – where citizens share a strong sense of collective solidarity and purpose, and broadly trust that the private resources they forgo to the state will be spent on public goods and services benefitting society as a whole – imbues taxation and redistribution policies with greater political support, while the realization of these goods and services themselves reinforces the vibrancy of the social contract. More broadly, the report recommends moving towards *equal protection* of all workers; ensuring that social assistance and basic quality services are provided *universally*; and enacting *progressivity* in a broad tax base that complements taxation of labor income with taxation of capital.[24] In a region otherwise known for its widespread support of a flat tax, such calls are new and thus not assured of widespread or sustained support.

Is it reasonable to expect that countries in Eastern Europe are generally capable of implementing policies providing equal protection to all on the basis of progressive taxation? To what extent would one expect citizens to be supportive of these ideas? Research provides some answers to these questions. Vibrant social contracts require governments capable of doing the difficult administrative work of both collecting revenue fairly and spending it equitably. Reducing inequality requires doing these tasks reliably, at scale, for all, which in turn requires high-capability public institutions. Drawing on cross-sectional time-series data from twenty-one countries in Central and Eastern Europe, Petrova (2020) shows that the quality of government affects the extent to which the state is capable of collecting and redistributing fiscal resources. Countries with higher levels of corruption, bureaucratic inefficiency, and weak enforcement of the rule of law are associated with lower levels of redistribution. That countries with higher levels of electoral participation are associated with higher relative redistribution, all things equal, leads her to conclude that the reason for this is that governing elites might fear being penalized for not curbing inequality.

This study also explores the supply and demand side of the redistribution process. On the supply side, Petrova finds that poor governance directly affects the redistribution process by hindering countries' ability to allocate funds to redistribution and deliver them to their beneficiaries. Poor governance thus contributes to inequality, she concludes, either by shaping individual preferences for social protection or by altering political actors' calculations about the costs and benefits of social reforms. Unlike earlier studies, which blame lower redistribution on the lack of public support for the welfare state, Petrova's examination of Eastern European countries finds no evidence of existing demand-oriented perspectives, and only weak evidence for arguments that poor governments undermine trust in state institutions and thereby decrease popular support for state-sponsored redistribution. She does find evidence, however, that higher ethnic fragmentation inhibits redistribution. These findings broadly align with those of Besley (2020), whose model, based on results from the European Values Survey, posits that governments lacking constraints will tend to disappoint their civic-minded and tax-compliant citizens, leading over time to an erosion in civic culture. Such erosion can be curtailed by making elites more accountable to their citizens – by protecting open media, promoting greater civic participation, and conducting regular performance audits.

Deaton 2020), reflecting "a long-term and slowly unfolding loss of a way of life" – have been especially high in rural, white working-class communities, taking lives at a rate that is lowering national life expectancy (a first for a historically rich country);[26] and poor minority groups (such as First Nations and African Americans) have been afflicted with Covid-19 at levels vastly disproportionate to their representation in the population (Tai et al. 2021).[27] Such cases stem from, among other factors, historical and contemporary political dynamics that have led the United States to currently rank 175th in the world – tied with Gambia – in terms of the "health-care access" it provides its citizens (Cameron et al. 2019: 180, 303). Enduring racial discrimination, rising inequality, and increasingly concentrated corporate power (Philippon 2019) enable the interests of financial elites to routinely prevail over the welfare of the most vulnerable. When one compares how effectively Europe and the United States respond to poverty, and explores the underlying reasons for the contrast between them, one discovers a social contract characterized by "a world of difference" (Alesina and Glaeser 2004).

In low- and middle-income countries, how such political economy dynamics play out over time also has enormous consequences for the well-being of the poor. As we noted above, for a country to reduce its rate of extreme poverty below 3 percent it must first attain a median level of income of at least around $1,600 (as Kyrgyz Republic did in 2002).[28] Indeed, *no country has ever eliminated extreme poverty without first attaining a median level of national wealth no less than $1,600.* But if Kyrgyz Republic (circa 2002) is the "floor," one can also observe a "ceiling": Bulgaria (in 2015), for example, did not reduce extreme poverty below 3 percent until it attained a median per capita level of economic development of over $5,200[29] – a more than threefold difference in national wealth. Clearly some poor countries are much better than others at generating inclusive economic growth – growth that benefits its poorest citizens. What explains this difference? Part of the explanation may reside in the structural nature of the growth process itself in particular countries; for now, we consider the role of politics and implementation issues, and in particular the nature of state–society relations.

How different types of social contract shape economic growth and poverty reduction

Promoting and enriching a vibrant social contract matters for its own sake – it is intrinsically important for elected governments to uphold their oaths of office, for citizens to participate in the everyday life of their community – but it is also instrumentally important for promoting inclusive growth and poverty reduction. To enhance "good governance," it is helpful to broadly distinguish between the extent to which governments are willing and able to implement an inclusive development agenda, focusing in particular on those states that are seemingly "unwilling" and/or "unable" to do so. In practice, of course, this analytical distinction is often blurred, with considerable variation between sectors, levels of government, and subnational areas, including changes over time. Even so, the very existence of this wide variation in willingness and ability to govern effectively for all is an empirical reality that needs to be documented, explained, and learned from.

Governments are likely to be *unwilling* to implement an inclusive, pro-poor policy agenda under two primary circumstances. First, when political contests between powerful rival factions become so intense that they prove unresolvable, with "winners" seeking primarily to secure rents for their exclusive use (often at the direct expense of others) and to retain their grip on power. In such circumstances, each party/group perceives itself to be engaged in a zero-sum game in which any concession to their rivals is experienced as an existential loss. In these circumstances, the state assumes monopoly control of the use of force, but it is entirely captured by the most dominant group, which directs the resources, rules, and any remaining veneer of credibility of the state (e.g., by having secured power through an election). Such actions are undertaken almost entirely in the service of legitimizing, protecting, and advancing the dominant group's interests, often at the direct expense of any other group, especially a non-elite group, that dares to even minimally challenge it.

Second, a pro-poor policy agenda is also unlikely to be supported when a dominant political faction succeeds in casting preferential economic responses for the poor as an unwarranted "distortion" of the "natural" or "efficient" workings of "free markets," as an exercise that creates "perverse incentives" for the poor, discouraging them from diligence, thrift, and adopting appropriate "pro-social behaviors" (e.g., reducing teen pregnancy, staying in school), all while enmeshing them in a debilitating "culture of dependency." Such charges are especially directed to those deemed to be the "undeserving poor" (those with "bad moral character"; Katz 2013), as opposed to the "deserving poor" (orphans, widows). Such arguments are common today, but have been made at least since the introduction of the world's first systematic poverty-reduction program, the English Poor Law, in the mid-1500s, and especially when it was substantially revised under the influence of Malthus in 1834, becoming in time the precursor to the modern welfare state of the post-World War II period (Lees 1998; Sherman 2001; Cooper and Szreter 2021). From a political economy perspective, it is perhaps not surprising that such views are often articulated by those whose *interests* align with maintaining the status quo; but key to consolidating such views into a broad-based and durable social contract is the emotional resonance and certain moral appeal of the *idea*.

Let us address each of these alternatives in turn. If their primary concern is maintaining power for the purpose of personal gain and security, governments are unlikely to be willing to enact even the most basic broad-based policy agenda. In many countries in the Horn of Africa, for example, everyday life for several decades has been mediated not by a functioning "social contract" but by a volatile "political marketplace" (de Waal 2015) in which competing elites use the pretext of elections to purchase and consolidate power, extracting revenue from citizens with little regard for whether these funds should be used to provide schools, roads, and water. As a recent World Bank report notes, in Somalia the "nascent political settlement holding the country together is fragile and under strain ... Between 2010 and 2020, there have been over 11,000 reported organized violent events. This translates to over three violent attacks a day every day of the year" (2020b: 7–8). Even so, it is important to stress that a weak or fragile state need not be synonymous with absent governance or futile efforts to improve (Menkhaus 2007; Hagmann and Hoehne 2009); the strategic cultivation and deployment of political will can pay off. For example, despite appearances, in Somalia (which remains the world's second-most "fragile state"), an array of informal service providers have emerged in recent years to deliver services ranging from water and roads to telecommunications and security – imperfectly, to be sure, but sometimes with remarkable effectiveness in the poorest urban communities. Civil society actors and the private sector have played a key role in these initiatives, but the state can also point to legitimate accomplishments,

> including the clearing of al-Shabaab from the capital Mogadishu and the capital city's ensuing economic boom, the implementation of a federal system of governance, two peaceful transfers of power following indirect elections in 2012 and 2017, gradual improvements in capacity building at all levels of government, and a successful civil society, government, and international response to the severe drought of 2017 that prevented what looked to be a serious famine. Somalia also normalized its relations with international financial institutions earlier this year [2020] for the first time in thirty years upon achievement of major milestones in terms of state building efforts. (World Bank 2020b: 10; see also World Bank 2017b)

In the least happy circumstances – especially in states where violence has been so endemic for so long that moments and spaces for exerting constructive leadership are at best likely to be fleeting – calling for such states to exert greater "political will" may seem hopelessly inadequate, even naive.

Violence has long been a pervasive and deadly reality in parts of Latin America, with local governments in certain areas of Mexico (to this day) and Colombia (until recently) seemingly unwilling to contain it because they themselves are sponsors and beneficiaries of the violence (see Kleinfeld 2018). A similar dynamic captures life in many favelas in Brazil, where the police often act in concert with rather than in opposition to the criminal gangs and drug traffickers that "govern" this space. Larkins concludes her extensive examination of the political dynamics of violence in the favelas by arguing that the criminal justice system is actively complicit in this violence and the everyday subjugation of the poor:

> The police enable the ongoing power of traffickers through corruption and through alienation of the favela population. BOPE [Battalion of Special Operations, an arm of the state] is a source of violent spectacle that does not serve to correct the failings of the police but rather works to reenact them in a different form. Prisons close the circle ... The prison is a place of punitive violence against the poor ... a stage for the enactment of performative spectacles of state punishment ... a place for the [drug] traffic to flex its muscle. (2015: 79)

From the perspective of advancing development, poverty reduction, and inclusive growth, such a state becomes part of the problem, even as it must eventually, somehow, become part of the solution; it seeks not to advance the welfare of an entire population by enacting policies that protect basic rights, enhance the productivity of its people and places, and increase the effectiveness and reach of key public services, but to consolidate the exclusive dominance and interests of the prevailing elite group.[30]

Violent conflict is the most consequential failure of a broken, or perhaps never-formed, social contract. A defining characteristic of the modern state is that it has a monopoly on the legitimate use of physical force; that is, the state alone – not citizens' militias, not religious groups, anarchists, gangs, or private contractors – has the power to coerce citizens, by force if necessary, to comply with its demands. Such power, of course, can be abused and thus needs corresponding counter-vailing political, social, and legal mechanisms to minimize the likelihood of this happening (Fox 2020). More problematic perhaps are the steps that might need to be taken, preceding or as part of peace settlement negotiations, to restore to the state its monopoly on violence – steps which may entail, for example, granting senior posts in the new government to individuals who held prominent leadership positions in opposition groups.[31] But the absence of a monopoly on the legitimate use of physical force, and the ensuing violent conflict to which it so often gives rise – especially if that conflict coalesces into a civil war – is likely to have devastating and enduring consequences for the well-being of the poor. As Mueller and Techasunthornwat argue, from an empirical standpoint, poverty reduction efforts often fail in areas "plagued by conflict ... But it has to be kept in mind that the much better identified micro literature finds dramatic effects of conflict exposure on physical and mental health, education levels and asset evaluations ... [I]t is entirely realistic that intense conflict ... is responsible for a population suffering from reduced human capital and low investments for years after the violence has stopped" (2020: 14–15).

Broadly speaking, governments are *unable* to implement their policy agenda when they lack the financial resources and/or organizational capability to do so, or simply face overwhelming external forces (e.g., regional wars, mass inflows of migrants, volatile commodity prices) they cannot reasonably contain. In principle such governments may wish to pursue an ambitious development agenda, the technical quality of the constituent policies may be exemplary, they may be governed by leaders whose motives are genuinely public-minded, and the policies they promote may enjoy broad political support. But if the financial and human resources are simply not available, or the organizations tasked with transforming sound and supported policy into lived reality are just not able to do so, then widespread disappointment and frustration will surely follow, including the very legitimacy of any reform process, which is highly likely to entail making costly trade-offs. In such circumstances, the state notionally presides over territory and people, but is simply "stretched too thin" – it cannot do the work expected of it, the most consequential effect of this being its inability to ensure the basic security of all persons and property.

In the absence of such a presence, law and order (such as it is) may become whatever local militarized groups deem it to be: at best, such groups may be relatively benign, enjoying some legitimacy to the extent they ensure basic order (perhaps on a fee-for-service basis); at worst, they routinely act arbitrarily, capriciously, or in their own self-interest, extorting exorbitant rents from vulnerable populations, and remaining accountable only to themselves. Here, a similar implementation logic applies to "the state" itself: unable to reliably pay and monitor its own agents, local justice "officials" become merely one actor among many vying for dominance, revenue, and control. The American "wild west" in the nineteenth century was such a place, and Ghana (for example) is perhaps an example today: lives and livelihoods remain precarious for the poor, but a measure of good fortune (consistent health, mild weather), social solidarity (community support), legal consistency, and personal diligence ensure that basic needs are met, that modest medium-run plans can reliably be enacted, and that young people can reasonably expect to experience at least modest welfare "improvement."

Conflict in such situations may not take the form of widespread or systematic violence, but it is highly likely to be a constant presence, in part because the very processes of development itself are disruptive and contentious (Barron et al. 2011). By design and definition, development is about change, and changes to the "rules of the game" – e.g., how order is maintained, disputes are addressed, power is legitimized, land is managed, and jurisdictional boundaries are set – is bound to create conflict, especially when different *types* of partially understood rules co-exist at the same time and place[32] (a phenomenon known as legal pluralism[33]). Educating children, for example, gives them literacy, numeracy, and analytical skills that enable them to apprehend the world in ways that may be vastly different from those of their illiterate parents; it may enable them to explore a wider array of employment options in far-away places, where they will likely meet, conduct business with, and encounter the religions (or lack of religion) of very different people. Learning the language of rights, contracts, and science is likely to give these children vastly different normative understandings of how the world works, how one lives a meaningful life, what constitutes justice and fairness, the priority one accords to upholding personal, familial, community, and professional obligations, how much discretionary "choice" one has to determine intimate partners, political affiliations, gender roles, and participation in cultural rites of passage. These evolving differences in the number and types of rules systems, when combined with the absence of credible procedures for arbitrating between them, become a tinderbox for pervasive everyday conflict. Echoing the empirical findings reported earlier in this chapter, "[t]he primary problem of politics," Huntington famously concluded, "is the lag in the development of political institutions behind social and economic change" (1968: 15).

Beyond conflict, the price of weak governance is deep inefficiencies, endemic corruption, and widespread frustration borne of persistent gaps between people's expectations and everyday lived experience, all of which undermine the coherence and credibility of the social contract. Over time, such weaknesses lead to heightened levels of instability, uncertainty, and flows of refugees (who are often the poorest and most vulnerable people of all, few of whom can be adequately accommodated). Lack of resources and administrative capability to do even basic tasks at an acceptable level means there is little opportunity to gain the capacity needed to address unexpected/unanticipated major shocks and to make credible long-term plans. Such challenges are compounded by weak data collection and curation, which compromises the state's capacity to design, implement, and assess effective pro-poor policy, and to manage hard trade-offs in ways perceived to be just, legitimate, and equitable, especially by those who "lose" when such decisions are made. A weak state and fragile social contract also renders a society vulnerable to the siren songs of populism – to politicians and civic leaders making emotionally resonant promises that can't be kept, and that widen rather than narrow social/economic divisions (e.g., "real citizens" versus "foreigners," rivals as "enemies," etc.) – and to authoritarianism (responding to uncertainty and discontent by suppressing the media, promulgating false information, and promoting rule *by* law rather than the rule *of* law) (Levitsky and Ziblatt 2018).

The clear challenge for those states unwilling and/or unable to implement strategies for promoting inclusive growth and reducing extreme poverty is to build more effective and accountable public institutions. This book obviously cannot provide comprehensive answers to these vexing questions, but in the sections that follow it seeks to shine some light on the mechanisms by which political dysfunctionality endures, and offer some analytical insights into why, in certain circumstances, pro-development reform has been able to be initiated, expanded, and sustained. Positive change can and has happened in seemingly unlikely circumstances, reversing situations where governments had for many years appeared both unwilling and unable to reduce entrenched political violence – in Bihar, India, and the city of Medellín, Colombia, for example. If such situations are exceptional, then perhaps seeking to build the administrative capability for pro-poor policy implementation in states that currently seem "unable" to do so is the more promising place to start; in either situation, however, responding more effectively is likely to require new approaches by governments and development agencies alike.[34]

Before exploring some of the dynamics behind why certain states in developing countries have found ways to be both willing and able to consistently deliver a pro-poor development agenda, while many others have not, it helps to consider an example of a longstanding and vibrant social contract in action: how the state of Kerala (India) responded to a novel but potentially existential threat (Covid-19).

Box 1.2 Responding effectively to the coronavirus: a vibrant social contract in Kerala

In India, the state of Kerala exemplifies the importance of the social contract for understanding how policy choices combined with effective implementation can have powerful long-term effects on poverty reduction. As Drèze and Sen (1995) have long documented, investing in basic education and health care for all has been a political priority in Kerala over many decades, but also one driven and maintained by sustained advocacy from civic organizations. Such investments are both intrinsically important and drivers of human capital across the income spectrum, but they are also products of deep reservoirs of trust and collective solidarity on which leaders can call during a crisis, such as that posed by a pandemic. In March 2020, Kerala – along with the rest of the world – faced such a crisis, with the emergence and rapid spread of the novel coronavirus. From one perspective, as Heller (2020) argues,

> Kerala's population density, deep connections to the global economy and the high international mobility of its citizens, [meant] it was primed to be a hotspot. Yet not only has the State flattened the curve ... it has also rolled out a comprehensive Rp. 20,000 crore (~USD 26.45 million) economic package before the Centre even declared the lockdown. Why does Kerala stand out in India and internationally?

Because, Heller argues, Kerala has long forged a robust social contract between the state and its citizens, with the pandemic subjecting it to a severe robustness check:

> Taming a pandemic and rapidly building out a massive and tailored safety net is fundamentally about the relation of the state to its citizens. From its first Assembly election in 1957, through alternating coalitions of Communist and Congress-led governments, iterated

cycles of social mobilization and state responses have forged what is, in effect, a robust social democracy.

The recent coronavirus pandemic, Heller continues, is akin to

a physical exam of the social body, and never has public trust been put to a greater test. In democracies, compliance must be elicited. Asking citizens to stay at home, to give up work, and to trust that the individual sacrifices they make now are essential to preserving the well-being of the community going forward is never easy to do and especially not against an invisible enemy. Trust is hard to measure, but survey work ... recently conducted in 10 Indian cities that included Kochi [the capital of Kerala], shows that across a wide range of measures, and across all classes, castes and religions, Malayalees [citizens of Kerala] have extremely high levels of trust in both their institutions and locally elected local representatives. This, more than anything, points to the robust nature of Kerala's social compact.

Creating, changing, and strengthening the social contract: how can the past guide the present?

In recent years there has been increasing recognition that development outcomes are powerfully shaped by state–society relations, which in turn are products of long-run historical processes (e.g., North et al. 2009). As important as this general principle of "learning from history" may be, however, there are multiple ways in which "lessons from the past" can be invoked – and indeed are invoked, in deeply consequential ways – to inform development policy and practice today (Woolcock et al. 2011). *How* one engages with the past has a powerful influence on the kinds of lessons one draws from it. If one requires stringent econometric standards of "causality" to be met in order to take seriously claims about the influence of the past on the present, for example, then a particular kind of "lesson" for policy is likely to be inferred. A veritable explosion of impressive historical research over the last two decades by economists offers compelling verification of the highly consequential and enduring effects of colonialism, and the legacies of different types of colonial regimes on different kinds of state–society relations today.[35] Such research makes clear that the nature and extent of the social contract in developing countries in the early twenty-first century has long roots, and confidently seeks to contribute to contemporary development policy (see Nunn 2020) – but rarely in actionable ways.

Politically, of course, there are other ways to read the past and to find reasons or justifications for policy choices in the present. Every country needs to have a coherent, credible, and compelling national narrative that defines what it is, what values it stands for, who exactly constitutes "us" (and, by extension, "them"), and how the country came to be in its current situation. It also needs to explain how the country has fared over time in comparison with itself and with its neighbors or rivals, and thus broadly inform what needs to be done in order for the country to move in a new or "better" direction. In the hands of very different leaders and political ideologies, this narrative will be told in very different ways, with the past selectively mined (or shamelessly invented) in ways that vindicate, embody, and amplify it. In one sense, such an approach to history cynically embodies a stance of "policy-based evidence," one that most practitioners instinctively (and rightly) resist, but it must nonetheless be taken seriously: every country has a national narrative, as does every political party within it (including those in democracies); indeed, every organization (including multi-lateral development agencies) has a narrative about itself. The challenge is to recognize the political and sociological imperative for having such a story – to lend political support, enhance morale, and inform a shared sense of collective purpose, to legitimize the connection between ends and means – even as one supports independent efforts to verify the accuracy of its claims. From a practical standpoint, development strategies that are inconsistent with the prevailing national narrative are unlikely to gain traction, especially if they entail reforms that will likely span multiple political cycles, elections, and administrations; those crafted in ways that appeal to broader constituencies and a shared national narrative stand a much better chance (see Ariadharma and Purnomo 2018).

The prominence and importance of national narratives for shaping domestic development policy is perhaps most apparent in the manner in which they are used to account for that country's encounter with "modernity" and its discontents. Beginning in the nineteenth century, but accelerated by events leading to the end of the colonial era in the mid-twentieth century and the advent of the Cold War, the terms on which leaders of newly independent countries engaged with their citizens (their identities, religions, and cultures), and with development agencies, multinational companies, and other countries, became powerfully shaped by their understanding of modernity, their enthusiasm for whether and how (and how fast) their country should itself become "modern," or engage with only those aspects it deemed desirable, or perhaps reject it entirely (Bayly 2004, 2018). Governance was thus enacted at the nexus of a rapidly changing social contract – i.e., of competing ideas, ideals, and administrative imperatives stemming from diverse understandings of what modernity is and does, in the process shaping policy and practice on topics ranging from national language(s), dress codes, social identity, and education (especially the teaching of history) to land management, agricultural practices, gender roles, foreign policy, rights to free speech and association, and the nature of state/religion relations.

Whether following a capitalist or a socialist path, newly independent countries, with the assistance of development agencies, became bound to craft, implement, and assess interventions of all kinds on the basis of "high-modern" administrative tools (surveys, censuses, plans, logframes, budgets, evaluations) that inexorably imposed uniformity on heterogeneity. In the process, they sought to "render legible" as fixed and uniform entities social categories that might otherwise be vastly more contingent and fluid (e.g., identity, caste; see Dirks 2001). Most conspicuously, they sought to transform "tradition" (indigenous religions, customary justice, nomadic life, folk medicine, illiteracy) into "modern" practices and sensibilities – adherence to a world religion (or none), rule of law, urban settlement, industrialization,[36] medical science, schooling (Scott 1998). Deference to such "technologies of rule" (Mitchell 2002; Hodge 2007) for determining problems and providing solutions (in the form of "projects" and "policy reform") left little space for substantive engagement with politics (Ferguson 1990). Adopting such administrative practices, however, secured legitimacy for leaders by conveying to citizens and the world their country's diligent adherence to emerging global norms of economic and social "progress," and the means by which it would be realized.[37] The resolution of competing claims surrounding these issues changed over time, sometimes with dramatic consequences – as reflected in the iconic photographs of everyday life in Kabul and Tehran in the early 1970s, as compared with such life thirty years earlier ... and indeed thirty years later.[38]

For some countries – such as those that were once at the epicenter of former empires (e.g., Hungary, Turkey, Russia, Persia), or on key trading routes (Mongolia), or in which religion has historically played a prominent role in shaping national identity (Iran, Afghanistan, India, Pakistan), or have experienced sustained economic decline (Venezuela, Zimbabwe, Argentina) – the dominant narrative in recent years has sought to explain their challenges while also charting a credible path back to prominence and "respect," even "greatness." This narrative may concede that certain aspects of modernity are necessary and desirable (reason, engineering, technology) while rejecting other aspects they frame as alien and thus undesirable (secularism, liberal democracy, "moral decadence"). On this account, however, modernity was (and remains) a mostly undesirable infiltrator, a corruptor of values, a compromiser of authentic cultural expression, a seducer who distracted earlier generations of feckless leaders, leading them to abandon their heritage and compatriots, and be played for fools by shady foreigners (and the compromised citizens aligned with them). Whether in a stagnant poor country or a rich country increasingly conscious of its decline, such a narrative in the mouth of a confident orator can generate enormous emotional appeal and a wide following, irrespective of the extent to which it actually accords with the historical facts.

From the mid-twentieth century, an alternative narrative arc characterized those countries that remained economically poor even as they more eagerly embraced much of the modernity package, or at least the appearance of having acquired it. In such countries, especially those emerging from colonialism, modernity was regarded as both a means to and a defining end of development – i.e., successive leaders declared that "becoming modern" was a goal to which the nation should properly aspire (and emulate along the way), and this goal was itself best attained by adopting "modern" instruments, tools, sensibilities, and professional standards (as in, for example, Tanzania or Indonesia). Staying the course would enable a country to take its rightful and respected place in the community of nations. According to this version of the national narrative, if our country failed to "develop" it was either because (a) it failed to adopt modernity's technology, reason, values, and practices with sufficient vigor and rigor, or (b) it adopted (or were effectively forced to adopt) an exclusively "western" version of modernity, one alien and inauthentic to its distinctive heritage, identity, culture, and way of life; leaders stressed instead a desire for their country to become "modern" but in its own way, on its own terms, having arrived there via a process the country itself deemed legitimate.[39]

Both of these latter narratives have their own political and implementation challenges. For the first, the risk is that the rush to be modern will manifest itself in "reforms" hailed as successful that in reality amount to little more than camouflage and imitation, accomplishing merely the appearance of being modern (McGovern 2012) – for many young people in Cote d'Ivoire, for example, Newell (2012) argues that modernity has largely become a performative "bluff."

For the second, the challenge is creating and sustaining robust domestic deliberative forums that can do the difficult, time-consuming work of owning a reform process that may fail (embarrassingly so) or generate procedures and outcomes that fit poorly within (or are illegible to) the prevailing administrative categories by which donors define and measure success. Such is the intensity of such pressures that they may become a key reason why the first option – reforming by "looking like a state" rather than being one – becomes by default, if not design, the dominant manner in which reform is undertaken (Andrews et al. 2017). That such approaches are doomed to disappointment may explain why the implementation capability of public sector organizations has steadily declined in developing countries over the last quarter century.

How are development agencies – and citizens themselves – to engage with such narratives, and perhaps contribute to ones that inform a more inclusive development policy agenda? Doing so is hard because the structure and content of national narratives rely on different historiographies – i.e., different ways of explaining "who we are," "how we got where we are," and "where we want to go," informed by different types and sources of meaning and reasoning (Gauri et al. 2013). In such circumstances it is therefore very hard to challenge each other's views on the basis of "the evidence" because each approach has its own frame of reference for determining what counts as a question and what counts as an answer. This is also true for discerning the salience for development policy of different kinds of scholarship about the past, which are often grounded in different disciplinary norms and methodological practices, and upon which the very foundations, distinctiveness, and scholarly integrity of the disciplines themselves rest. What to do? Who might do it? On what basis? It is to these questions that we now turn.

–2–
Managing a Contentious World: Cooperation, Inclusion, Process Legitimacy

In the previous chapter, I argued that there were three different modalities of development: (i) the aspirations expressed and actions undertaken by countries, whether singularly or as part of a broader geopolitical dynamics, to enhance their prosperity and stature ("national development"); and, since the end of World War II, (ii) the emergence of multilateral and bilateral agencies and major foundations seeking primarily to support the aspirations and actions of these countries and peacefully mediate disputes between them ("big development"); complemented by (iii) discrete programs focused on enhancing the welfare of particular people (the poor, refugees, minorities, women) living in particular places, often enacted or championed by non-government organizations, domestic charities, and advocacy groups ("small development").

I also argued that the most apt metaphor for understanding development was as an "epic adventure" (Hirschman) – the human journey writ large and small, undertaken since the very existence of *Homo sapiens*, embraced (or resisted) for a myriad of noble and ignoble reasons in a variety of ways, informed and justified by all manner of commercial, political, technological, environmental, ideological, and religious imperatives. Sometimes the adventure ended well, other times disastrously; but in many respects any particular "ending" was and is only an interlude, a prelude to something else, the precise destination unknown.

Beginning in seventeenth-century England, "development" became global over the course of the long nineteenth century and fully intensified in the post-colonial period following World War II, in so doing becoming a distinctive and explicitly intentional form of human journey, one in which reason and resources are harnessed to move history itself, to presume that "the wealth of nations" can be created, sustained, and shared by all. To more fully appreciate this framing – the emergence of development and how three different forms of it came to comprise the logics within which it is undertaken today – we need to start with the beginning of humanity's epic adventure. Such adventures are told and recounted as stories, but then so are all the theories of development. If there is a danger in having access to only a single story (Adichie 2009), there is also a danger in having too many stories or none at all. We will encounter other stories of the development process along the way, but for present purposes I propose that development is best understood as a uniquely modern extension of humanity's epic adventure because of the vital role played by social institutions (i.e., groups, languages, religions, norms, rules, and laws).

Development as an "epic adventure"[1]

Recent research in population genetics is transforming our understanding of human prehistory and, in the process, demonstrating almost conclusively that all 7.4 billion of us are 99.9 percent genetically identical.[2] It shows that, some 2,500 generations (or 70,000 years) ago, our forebears – perhaps as few as a hundred – walked out of Africa and began an extraordinary journey that took them along various routes into (what is now) Europe, across Asia, down into Australia and throughout the Pacific islands,[3] while others headed north across the Bering Strait (when it was an ice bridge) into North and eventually South America. It's relatively clear *why* our forebears did this: they sought access to better food sources as their numbers grew, existing food stocks declined, and conflict intensified. But how *did* they do it, in ways no other species have? By inventing thousands of different social institutions – languages, religions, and informal rules systems – facilitating qualitative improvements in cognitive capacity, collective action, technological capability, and strategic cooperation. This enabled increasingly large groups to accomplish together – for better (enhancing navigation, technological innovation, trade, artistic creations) and for worse (enacting devastating wars, violent conquest, pandemics) – what had been previously unthinkable, let alone doable, by small, isolated, pre-lingual familial bands. Recent research suggests there was wide variation in the ways these larger human communities organized themselves (Graeber and Wengrow 2021); there was no single path along which the human journey unfolded. Even so, it was languages, religions, and rules systems (encompassed by social norms, or informal behavioral expectations) that were the social institutional "tools" by which the core familial unit – the sociological equivalent of the atom (Davis 2009) – was "scaled up" into political and economic organizations that in turn enabled exchange with strangers and negotiation with rivals. The subsequent "scaling down" of the family unit created the notion of the individual as a bearer of rights and responsibilities (consolidated during the Enlightenment but with a longer intellectual history; see Siedentop 2014). These fundamental shifts in ideas, social relations, and the bases of power, when combined with the contemporaneous advent of science, revolutionized humanity's technological, navigational, financial, and organizational capability – and hence also its military capability.

This intoxicating capacity to have seemingly "subdued" nature – the land, the sea, animals, and plants – led almost inexorably to the notion that this new knowledge and power could also be applied not merely to subdue humans but also to control history.[4] Sociology, as articulated by its "founder" Auguste Comte in the 1850s, was to be the "science of society," indeed the "crowning achievement" of science itself.

From this conceptualization, however, followed notions that different societies and social groups were at different stages of "civilization." How history itself was understood was also transformed, as were the processes by which group biographies were created and their origins recounted (Burrow 2008). By the late eighteenth century and early nineteenth, these contradictions between new assertions of liberty and human (or at least male) equality, on the one hand, and revisionist understandings of racial hierarchies on the other, came to a head, most graphically in the insidious practice of slavery. But these changes generated enormous contention across all aspects of society, not least among those whose stature, livelihoods, and interests were directly threatened by notions of liberty and equality, and by new sources of wealth, power, and prestige. In certain quarters, the nascent social sciences were invoked to mount a backlash against "modern" ideas – especially the notions of gender and racial equality – even as change was construed in quasi-evolutionary terms as a process by which humanity itself "improves" and "progresses" from savagery to barbarism to civilization. Such understandings had disastrous consequences for certain social groups (especially indigenous populations) deemed to be "backward" (or even sub-human).[5] Colonial expansion and conquest was justified in no small part by this logic.

The revolutions in Europe across the late seventeenth century to the early nineteenth fundamentally altered basic understandings of the formal rights, freedoms, and responsibilities of individuals (vis-à-vis other individuals, groups, and the state), the limits of state and religious authority, the pace and desirability of technological advance, and the scale and legitimacy of commercial activity (e.g., money-lending and free trade on the supply side, aspiration and consumerism on the demand side; de Vries 2008). The centrally disruptive process underpinning these changes was the steady expansion of capitalism and technological change, a "relentless revolution" (Appleby 2010) of "creative destruction" (Schumpeter 1983) which continues to unfold today. But how did this first era of sustained society-wide economic growth begin? Why did it do so in England – on a small, rain-soaked island on the periphery of the (then) world economy, whose inhabitants spoke an obscure mash-up language and lived under a strange, idiosyncratic legal system? How did it sustain itself there where previous "take-offs" elsewhere (Egypt, Central Asia, China) had petered out? Box 2.1 provides a potential answer: because, over the course of the seventeenth century, the English uniquely (a) forged new ideas about the desirability and possibility of material "improvement" by all members of society (Slack 2015[6]); (b) implemented, under the pioneering leadership of Elizabeth I, in response to the Black Death, history's first "development institution" (Smith 2011) – a national registration policy and the Poor Law, which together enabled the provision of financial resources to the poorest in times of need, thereby enabling labor mobility, promoting society-wide innovation, and eliminating famines (Cooper and Szreter 2021: 251–66); and (c) placed enforceable legal (constitutional) constraints on monarchical power (Pincus 2009). In short, centuries before there was an "Industrial Revolution," there was history's first (albeit unwitting) "national development" strategy.[7]

This first era of sustained economic growth and increasingly global integration, unfolding over the course of the "long" nineteenth century, came to a crushing end with World War I. The failure, in turn, to manage the war's aftermath (in part through the League of Nations) both delegitimized internationalism as a political project and brought on the further devastation of the Great Depression, and in its turn, World War II (Frieden 2020). Modernity's most powerful inventions – nation states, capitalism/communism, secular ideology, and rational bureaucracy – were transparently capable of total, complete, self-destruction. That the incidence and effects of major wars and financial crises have been vastly smaller in the post-World War II period is testament to the talents and persistence of leaders in the 1920s and 1940s who campaigned for, devised, and then implemented a new international architecture that salvaged both the idea and the practice of open trade, peace, social equality, and democracy, ensuring (so far) that the awesome powers of modernity have been mostly harnessed for the general enhancement of

Box 2.1 When and why was there an "Industrial Revolution" in England?

Historians have rightly noted that there have been multiple and early "modernities" (Wong 1997; *Daedalus* 1998, 2000; Starr 2013). It is beyond the scope of this book to summarize these initial periods of "development," or to explore the reasons why they (for the most part) did not endure – except to note that prevailing social and political institutions, threatened by new forms and sources of power, often played a central role.[8] This can be seen in recent research on the timing and origins of the Industrial Revolution in England, its very name asserting that there was a "revolution" – i.e., a decisive transformation – and that this transformation was driven by fundamental technological advances in "industrial" production. If asked when this Industrial Revolution took place, most people would likely say (something like) "With accelerating intensity over the course of the nineteenth century."

And they would be partly right – there clearly was a major acceleration in growth in England in the nineteenth century (and elsewhere), as Figure 2.1 below indicates. But recent advances in the quality and scope of data on European economic growth since the 1400s allows a potentially more interesting story to be told. Consider again Figure 2.1, which shows at least three other things. First, in the early 1600s, the Netherlands was roughly twice as rich as England and France (and probably everyone else) – if you were betting in 1620 which country would be pioneering economic growth in 1820, your money would surely be on the Netherlands. Second, England's economic take-off began in the mid-1600s and it rarely looked back: despite its numerous wars, England had roughly 150 years of steadily rising growth before its Industrial Revolution, while per capita income in the Netherlands was *lower* in 1820 than it had been in 1620 (and was prone to wild annual fluctuations). Third, all three countries experienced rapid growth across the nineteenth century, but France's "level of development" barely changed between 1400 and 1800 – 400 years! What explains these different growth trajectories? All three countries were imperial powers for much of this period, and tolerated domestic slavery with roughly similar degrees of intensity and legality, so these factors don't seem strong enough to explain the relative differences in their growth trajectories.

What *is* different is that, from 1500 to 1800 (and onwards, though in a greatly modified form following drastic cutbacks led by Thomas Malthus), England alone had a Poor Law – perhaps the world's oldest and longest-running welfare program; indeed, Smith (2011) explicitly suggests it was a bona fide "development institution." Championed by Elizabeth I in the aftermath of the Black Death, the Poor Law combined (a) widespread identity registration that was recognized across the country (a comprehensive system overseen by local parishes that, to this day, enables those with British ancestors to trace their genetic heritage with extraordinary detail and accuracy); and (b) universal access to a basic income (paid for via a local tax levied on the wealthy, who were persuaded to pay it on the self-interested basis that the non-destitute were likely to be healthier, more productive, and less unruly) that was mobile – that is, when workers moved, they could immediately claim benefits from the Poor Law in their new place of residence.[9] The upshot was twofold: (i) labor became relatively mobile, less bound by feudal arrangements that elsewhere restricted the poor to tight geographically constrained spaces, thus enabling workers to pursue employment opportunities where and when they became available; and (ii) workers were able to innovate, invent, and explore, safe in the knowledge that "failure" needn't mean destitution. One may not be able to formally demonstrate a direct causal link between the Poor Law and the timing and location of the Industrial Revolution, but both the uniqueness, comprehensiveness, and longevity of the Elizabethan Poor Law, and the empirical fact that the growth take-off in England occurred 150 years before the broader productivity revolution of the nineteenth century, places a high burden on those seeking to offer a better explanation. Indeed, Dutch historians themselves acknowledge that the *universal* nature of the English Poor Laws was what set them apart from every other European country from the sixteenth century onwards (van Bavel and Rijpma 2016).

In any event, using the categories introduced above, I am persuaded that this is almost certainly history's first (if unwitting) "national development" initiative – a systematic attempt by national leaders, at scale and over *centuries*, to recognize the identity of every citizen, to facilitate their freedom of movement, and to provide them with a minimum level of economic security for weathering hard times. (I say "unwitting" because the Poor Law was not launched with the long-run goal of promoting "development" or a "productivity revolution" – these were the unintended consequences of what began as a shared moral commitment to providing dignity and material support to society's most vulnerable members in the aftermath of a pandemic and famines.)

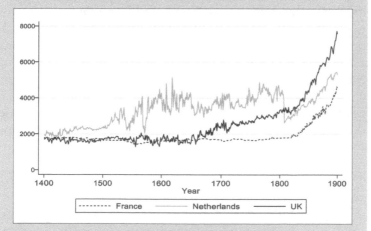

Figure 2.1 GDP per capita income, 1400–1900 (in 2011$)

Source: Author's construction, from Maddison Project Database, version 2020. See Bolt and Van Zanden (2020), https://www.rug .nl/ggdc/historicaldevelopment/maddison/releases/maddison-project -database-2020

human welfare.[10] Good fortune and patience also played an important role (it was never self-evident or inevitable that the Cold War would end relatively peacefully), but even so, as the "early modernity" of China in the sixteenth century showed, as the early twentieth-century experience of Europe showed, and as certain countries today (e.g., Venezuela, Zimbabwe) still show, modernity's gains can all unravel, quickly and violently. There is nothing certain or inexorable about human "progress," and its attainment nearly always comes at a high price for those least well-placed to respond to its demands, as climate change today amply demonstrates.

In short, "development" – understood as widespread peace, democracy, social equality, clean water, safe food, public health systems, education, and shared prosperity – is a marvelous, wondrous, deeply precarious accomplishment.[11] But in the early decades of the twenty-first century, this *sensibility* of how the modern world came to be is not how the "problem" of development is – and its corresponding "solutions" are – generally understood. We are today more aware of the alternative paths that could have been taken at any number of historical junctures, of how inherently disruptive modernity has been (and continues to be) for prevailing ideas, political systems, and social institutional arrangements, and of how fraught with uncertainty anyone's actions to engineer "progress" necessarily are. Changing this requires not just a stronger historical sensibility among contemporary development professionals, but an appreciation of the enduring role of social institutions today, and the legitimacy they confer upon (or withhold from) the wrenching processes of change that development, in all its manifestations, entails.

"Process legitimacy" and development: forms, sources, and applications

A major reason why international development is humanity's greatest challenge, I have argued, is because there is often wide disagreement about its means and ends – i.e., what counts as "progress" or "improvement" for different groups, and how this will be achieved. Thus far we have focused primarily on the ends or goals being sought in the name of development, and the key actors involved in articulating, promoting, or providing them; in this section, I explore the challenges associated with establishing procedures for achieving these goals, whatever they may be, that are acceptable (enough) to all parties. For present purposes I call this aspect "process legitimacy." I address four aspects of process legitimacy in turn: why it matters, what forms and sources it takes, how competing forms are reconciled, and the empirical foundations on which claims associated with each of these rest. More formally, process legitimacy refers to the mechanisms and procedures by which change is brought about, and the extent to which these are regarded as sufficiently just, credible, and fair by all parties, but especially those who bear the highest costs. Process legitimacy is concerned with ensuring that development outcomes (the ends) are justified by the means sought to implement them, especially by those who may lose out (such as workers, traditional leaders, residents of a particular location) by the attainment of these outcomes (e.g., enhanced education, technology, infrastructure).[12]

1. Why process legitimacy matters

In his classic book *Why People Obey the Law*, Tom Tyler (2006) argues that people willingly comply with laws for two primary reasons: because their personal morality compels them to, and/or because they believe both the laws themselves and those enforcing them to be legitimate. In related work, drawing upon numerous empirical studies, he stressed that

> the key factor shaping public behavior is the fairness of the processes legal authorities use when dealing with members of the public. This reaction occurs both during personal experiences with legal authorities and when community residents are making general evaluations of the law and of legal authorities. The strength

and breadth of this influence suggests the value of
an approach to regulation based upon sensitivity to
public concerns about fairness in the exercise of legal
authority. (Tyler 2003: 283)

In this section, I extend this logic to the legitimacy of rules
systems more generally, using it to consider the manner in
which the development process may challenge and change
prevailing forms and sources of legitimacy (e.g., by introducing new mechanisms for determining resource allocation,
accountability, and contract enforcement),[13] and to explore
how the consolidation of legitimate processes for effectively
mediating increasingly complex issues is *itself* a defining
feature of development.

The case for taking process legitimacy seriously should be
relatively straightforward: the credibility of any mechanism
for resolving competing claims in life – from national elections
and corporate budget allocations to court decisions and
routine job applications – is central to ensuring that all parties
to the contest, especially those who are dealt unfavorable
outcomes, accept the result. For example, every election has
to be deemed "free and fair" by impartial observers in order
for the outcome to be formally recognized and be declared
to have upheld a sufficient measure of integrity.[14] Przeworski
famously defined democracy itself as simply "a system in
which parties lose elections" (1991: 10) – that is, a process
by which deeply consequential public losses are peacefully
accepted by those groups who failed to secure a sufficient
number of votes, because they believe the votes were properly
cast, counted, and verified.[15] Similarly, a defining feature
of the rule of law is that everyone who challenges the state
is entitled to "due process" (precisely because of the vast
differences in power between the claimants). More broadly,
we accept unfavorable outcomes in everyday life – not
getting into a first-choice college, being denied a loan from a
bank, having a grant application rejected, losing a sporting
contest – to the extent we believe those making the decisions
followed agreed-upon procedural rules, upheld agreed-upon
standards, and acted in good faith (despite potentially facing

powerful individual incentives or political pressure to do otherwise).

Process legitimacy can be secured in various ways (see next section), but the "work" legitimacy does is largely the same, namely ensuring that *how* things get done meets shared expectations, thereby enabling the means to justify the ends (as varied as the ends themselves may be).[16] In development, however, where *change* is explicitly and intentionally the central policy objective, changing the ends (e.g., improving learning, health practices, gender equity) is highly likely to also require changing the means (adoption of new classroom pedagogy, scientific medicine and agricultural practices, updated laws and social norms) (Smith et al. 2002). Introducing "new ways of doing things" to achieve development goals may or may not align with the prevailing ways of doing things; in the most extreme case, where "old" and "new" processes are inimical, extended periods of negotiation will likely be needed to create an interim mechanism that reconciles them (see below), lest extended conflict or a stalemate ensues. The full package of most development interventions – inclusion, gender equality, transparency, "meritocracy," science, accountability, human rights, evidence-based decision-making – may or may not accord with what is considered legitimate by national governments, let alone local communities.

More broadly, the development process requires all manner of complex trade-offs to be managed and contentions to be resolved, yet the necessary rules, standards, norms, and procedures for enabling these trade-offs to be made and enforced are routinely either absent, inadequate, contradictory, or compromised, thereby becoming part of the problem. It is widely recognized, for example, that all children everywhere need to complete at least ten years of effective learning (not merely ten years of attending school) in order to be minimally prepared for active participation in a modern economy and society; it is also widely recognized that children learn best in their native language. Yet for national learning objectives to be obtained at scale in any given country, it will likely require the medium of instruction to be a singular national language (or perhaps the two most widely spoken languages), thereby immediately placing at a great disadvantage those who do not speak the national language.

Moreover, for some groups (e.g., women), the very act of successfully attaining a formal education – or their children attaining such an education while they remain illiterate – may lead to assertive pushback from those threatened by a newly empowered group,[17] or a gradual breakdown in the everyday social cohesion of their community (see Box 2.2). In this sense, then, there are at least two levels at which process legitimacy is needed: first in initiating, prioritizing, and implementing the policy; second in sustaining it over time, in the face of both unintended social effects (e.g., a lack of employment opportunities in the local area for those with a newly acquired formal education) and overt resistance from those whose interests or values may be challenged by the policy's attainment (e.g., elders, religious authorities). (See also the related discussion below on "meta-rules": the rules that make it possible for otherwise different rules systems to co-exist or be harmonized.)

This matters for all aspects of development, but it is especially salient for *social* development issues precisely because identities, relationships, expectations, aspirations, and rules themselves are disruptively changed, no matter whether development efforts succeed (more/better schools, roads, hospitals, insurance) or fail (violent conflict, economic crisis, widespread corruption, environmental degradation, epidemics). Process legitimacy is central to navigating and negotiating these vexing challenges. Even if it is unreasonable to expect that procedures for addressing all these different development challenges can be anticipated ex ante or faithfully addressed in situ, and that the very existence of grievance redress mechanisms may raise expectations that may not be able to be met, it should not be unreasonable for development professionals to acknowledge from the outset that the goals they are promoting are, by design and definition, likely to be experienced as deeply disruptive, even overtly "destructive" (in the Schumpeterian sense; see also Aghion et al. 2020). As such, the inevitable concerns generated by this disruption should not be regarded as mere annoyances

Box 2.2 The social costs of development success

Development – by definition and design – changes how people live. The policies and practices invoked to bring this about, however, are mostly justified to the extent they achieve significant measurable progress towards the attainment of a narrow target or specific set of tangible goals; the secondary, longer-term, or unintended changes that accompanying the attainment of (let alone the failure to reach) the narrow goals are rarely considered. Put more formally, development changes an existing "social equilibrium" comprising many parts, all of them interdependent; when one narrow slice of one of those parts is moved – even positively, generating clear individual or aggregate welfare gains – it inherently changes everything else. Development is therefore inexorably disruptive; it is creative *and* destructive; it generates winners *and* losers; it is thereby contentious and alters prevailing power relations.

Consider Luther, a resident of a small town some 20 kilometers from Port Vila, the capital of the Pacific island nation of Vanuatu, a lower middle-income country. Luther is chief of the all-male village council, as was his father before him. Luther doesn't know when exactly he was born, since there exists no formal record of when or where he entered the world; he guesses that he is around forty-five, but people his age never celebrated birthdays when he was growing up, so it hasn't mattered much. Luther has five daughters by two different wives. He is disappointed he doesn't have a son – who will chair the village council when he is gone? – but he is also chair of the prestigious Regional Development Board and as such is proud to show visitors the two primary schools in his district, quick to stress to government officials that his eldest two daughters attend the regional high school, and to highlight that his wives – unlike those of his poorer neighbors – gave birth in hospitals.

However, at the end of another day spent reassuring anxious donors that he is indeed committed to gender equity and maintaining classroom enrollments, Luther candidly but quietly laments that while he is pleased that his daughters go to school and can now read and write – "their future depends on it," he concedes – it has come at a steep price. Luther and his fellow council elders never attended school and so they are illiterate; to his daughters, the inability of Luther and his generation to read even a newspaper headline or sign their name makes them seem simple, even fools. The pronouncements they make as village elders are taken less seriously with each passing year; the basis on which they resolve disputes seems increasingly arbitrary (or worse) to the rising generation; even the treasurer of the development council is unable to keep formal records of monies allocated to them, opening all board members to charges that they are "unaccountable." "How can you protect our land from being taken from us if you can't even read the contracts being offered by the mining companies?," Luther's daughters complain. "Why are our mothers not allowed to be on the village council? They are just as smart as you! Why do you keep making silly sacrifices to the gods? How can you possibly not even know how old you are?"

As he ponders the future, Luther steels himself against the likely reality that his educated daughters will choose a life vastly different from his own. He awaits the day when his daughters – unsatisfied with expectations that they should stay in the village, marry at a young age to a local boy chosen for them, and raise many children while maintaining the family's crops and animals – will announce that they want a "better life," a "career," a chance to "see the world," to "make something of themselves," and so will leave for Port Vila, or perhaps to take up work overseas as a domestic helper. This means they will probably never come back, will marry a foreigner, will raise children who know nothing of their parents' heritage and language, and will be unable to look after Luther in his sunset years. "It's all well and good that my daughters are getting educated," Luther concludes, "but we have lost our world; my generation has not entered another, yet my daughters are now in a strange new world, never to return. We are neither here nor there."

Source: Based on a field visit by the author

to be mitigated after the fact but instead as serious concerns needing to be addressed proactively as a necessary part of the development process.[18] Indeed, a constituent definition of development, in its fullest form, is that it incrementally builds robust administrative and judicial institutions able to manage the increasingly complex and contested tasks that successful development necessarily brings about.

2. Forms and sources of process legitimacy

Process legitimacy matters for both large and small development issues, but it comes in many forms derived from many difference sources. And when sufficiently different forms and sources of process legitimacy encounter one another – as they frequently do, in (for example) disputes over land use, agricultural practices, the management of common pool resources (water, fisheries), and maternal health – there is the potential for confusion, mistrust, and contention. What is deemed a legitimate process by one group may be anathema to another,[19] and what is regarded by a majority at a given point in time as legitimate (e.g., slavery) may become anathema over time.[20] Some primary forms and sources of process legitimacy include, but are not limited to:

a. *Technical expertise.* Deference is given to an individual or organization with recognized technical credentials as verified and enforced by a professional association (lawyers, scientists, accountants, engineers). The deployment of such skills may be especially important in situations of crisis or sustained uncertainty, where the limits of prevailing knowledge have been reached. Conditional on their legal mandate, most international development agencies prioritize and invoke technical expertise as the primary foundation on which their legitimacy to engage in client countries rests. Calling upon such professionals also provides a credible legal defense in the event that unfavorable outcomes ensue. Today's apparent "crisis" in the legitimacy of expertise (Nichols 2018), as manifest in divisive debates over the salience of climate change and policy responses to Covid, is a product of both the heightened pressure on experts to solve the world's increasingly complex problems *and* the inherent limits to what it is reasonable to expect any legitimate expert (or team of experts) to accomplish (Eyal 2019). Once the gap sufficiently widens between what citizens expect from experts and what they actually get – as is almost inevitable in an increasingly complex world – the credibility and legitimacy of genuine technical expertise in any form is vulnerable to populist pushback. So understood, development-as-disruption can fundamentally alter how different "epistemic communities" (i.e., groups sharing a common understanding of what counts as a question and what counts as an answer) regard how justice should be carried out, how public funds should be generated and spent, how the very basis of "expertise" itself is determined in a given situation. To be clear: technical expertise can and should be the basis for resolving technical problems, but such expertise inherently has its limits, and many key problems in development (and everywhere else) are not narrowly technical (such as resolving violent conflict). Doubling down on technical expertise as the basis for asserting the legitimacy of development initiatives *in general*, and for resolving its attendant challenges, risks exacerbating the problem if the problem itself is not primarily technical.

b. *Designated authority figures.* Legitimate development outcomes may be obtained when decision-making powers are granted to a person who has won (e.g., via an election) or otherwise attained (e.g., through extensive experience or inheritance) the right to make key decisions. The US president, for example, can by law personally negotiate trade deals with foreign countries; autocrats too may declare that their proclamations (e.g., to start a war) are legitimate precisely because such powers have been granted to (or seized by) them; a designated village elder (not an independent jury) may be called upon to decide guilt or innocence in a local criminal case (e.g., rape), where the paramount concern in reaching a just and legitimate outcome centers on upholding the honor of the group, not the rights of the individual victim. All three of these cases may yield outcomes that external observers regard as abhorrent but that are nonetheless regarded as legitimate by those within a given political, cultural, or religious jurisdiction. The potentially vast gap between these different forms and sources of legitimacy can generate potentially lethal conflict, or at a minimum create considerable ethical dilemmas for those seeking to find common ground by making concessions and compromises, or by finding it necessary (e.g., in order to uphold international laws and agreements to which a country is a signatory) to impose a particular solution on a particular group.

c. *Established (legal) precedent.* When a given case is deemed to be an instance of an earlier episode for which a verdict was reached (a "decided case"), the earlier decision can provide a basis for resolving the present case; the law (common law in particular) derives much of its power and legitimacy from being the accepted repository for such cases (Bingham 2010; Pirie 2021). Attempts by courts to overturn "settled law" can thereby be regarded as deeply illegitimate by some, and as the very point of politics by others; similarly, it is the ability of certain laws to become entrenched (Starr 2019) – i.e., to be resistant to reform – that is both a feature and a vulnerability of democratic societies. Good and bad laws alike can become entrenched for good and bad reasons, just as they can be changed. Either way, prevailing law provides the basis for the legitimacy on which difficult decisions pertaining to the status of novel cases are assessed.

d. *Agreed-upon procedural rules.* Within a given political or social jurisdiction, and when enabled by a mandate, formal and informal rules can be called upon to determine how decisions will be made. Administrative law is only the most visible manifestation; *Robert's Rules of Order* is another, as is (say) the World Bank's Articles of Association and its Staff Manual. Whether completing routine tasks (applying for promotion) or navigating complex or contentious issues (adjudicating whether a certain staff behavior – e.g., serving on a corporate board – constitutes a conflict of interest), situations that could otherwise become chaotic, dominated by the most powerful, or prone to arbitrary outcomes, can be readily resolved if there is clear access to agreed-upon procedural rules providing a transparent basis on which decisions can be reached. Such decisions are deemed legitimate because they fall within the purview of a clear and specific jurisdiction, which itself is understood to be governed by rules to which constituent members have given their prior consent.

e. *Tradition or custom.* But many rules guiding our lives aren't formally specified, and not all of them can or should be, since (i) there is a distinctiveness to each case, (ii) our cognitive "bandwidth" is necessarily limited, and (iii) humans would be much less interesting if everything about them could be fully "figured out."[21] As such, we learn all manner of everyday social norms and routines to help guide behavior in the present moment;[22] these are embodied in traditions and customs representing "the way things are done here," becoming procedures for decision-making whose legitimacy stems from them being shared and having stood the test of time. But traditions and customs can sit awkwardly with science and settled law. Among Australia's various aboriginal tribes, for example, dreamtime narratives about a group's origins – and thus that group's identity, the legitimacy of any individual's membership in the group, and that individual's obligation to uphold the group's specific rights and responsibilities – are ontologically orthogonal to the scientific findings stemming from genetic testing, which affirms via DNA analysis the existence of links to groups in South Asia and further back to the groups who made the earliest migrations out of Africa. (Similarly, some First Nations groups in the Americas are offended by scientific claims regarding their origins.) These contrasting approaches to understanding a group's origins are, to use Scott's (1998) term, largely "illegible" to one another; the foundations of their respective forms and sources of legitimacy seem mutually exclusive, even as they are of existential importance to each.

f. *Religious, philosophical, and/or ideological principles.* Prevailing laws, rules, and norms for collective decision-making often reflect a larger collation of ideas and practices grounded in theological and/or political doctrine. In certain forms, the legitimizing power of such codified doctrines (from crusades and purity norms to communism and democracy) is of a magnitude that, historically, it has been something that millions of people are willing to torture, kill, and die to protect or promote. More helpfully, moral principles, no matter their origins, can also inform and sustain noble behavior, enabling individuals and groups to stand firm in the face of abuse, oppression, and exclusion, of physical intimidation, peer pressure, or lucrative inducements to conform. When such principles are enshrined in global commitments such as the Universal Declaration of Human Rights, they mark a genuine historical advance; when ratified by a given national government, they provide legitimacy for citizens of that country to highlight subsequent infringements. At the local level, inclusive deliberative forums can be a political space wherein diverse views on contentious issues are aired and (potentially) resolved, thereby imbuing the final outcome with broader legitimacy precisely because it was reached via a mechanism charged with doing this difficult work (see Gibson and Woolcock 2008, and Rao 2019).

g. *Instrumental efficacy.* An initially difficult or controversial societal change – such as decentralization or gender equality – may, over time, earn legitimacy because it achieves the welfare-enhancing goals promised by its advocates. Here, the ends themselves come to justify the means, at least when the ends are perceived to be widely and instrumentally favorable. Such a pact, however, is politically vulnerable: Suharto's governing policies in Indonesia, for example, which included flagrant corruption, were tolerated as long as the economic pie expanded; his legitimacy (and presidency) collapsed when a regional financial crisis led to an epic economic crisis, exposing the political rot for what it was. Similar arguments are made today to assert that the legitimacy of actions by autocratic governments – and citizens' willingness to tolerate civic repression and omnipresent surveillance – is only as strong as its sustained economic growth; were the latter to implode, the argument goes, the ensuing crisis would expose and exacerbate societal fault-lines.[23] Recent research suggests that, in fragile states, "performance-based legitimacy" (Levi 2018) can, at least under certain conditions, be an important foundation on which initial material gains are consolidated. This is also the argument for securing "quick wins" in the early stages of contentious policy reforms whose hoped-for gains are only likely to be secured in the medium run: uncertainly pertaining to the legitimacy of these reforms can be at least partially assuaged if the initial experience is sufficiently positive. (By extension, early losses can prove fatal if the dominant ensuing narrative becomes one of wholesale policy failure.)

h. *Alignment of proclamations and actions.* The legitimacy of difficult policy changes undertaken in the name of promoting development, especially when they are perceived to be championed by external agents, requires an alignment of the principles and behaviors of those external agents (such as the World Bank or a donor government). If the values these agents claim to espouse – and call upon the recipients of their resources/expertise/largesse to enact (such as transparency, merit-based hiring, and accountability) – are inconsistent with how these agents themselves behave, then it should hardly be surprising if recipients accord little legitimacy to such claims.[24] As recent scholarship has argued, however, development failures in Eastern Europe (Krastev and Holmes 2019) and Afghanistan (O'Toole 2021) are in no small part a product of perceived gross hypocrisy on the part of the West, which has greatly compromised both its own legitimacy and the legitimacy of the difficult steps it asks others to take. The West claims, for example, to be a champion of human rights, international law, and the "rule of law," yet shamelessly tortures political prisoners, absolves itself of war crimes, and has initiated wars of choice absent UN approval (Iraq); it claims to promote democracy, yet its own political and financial systems are rife with loopholes, kickbacks, and special deals for the well-connected; it claims to be promoting poverty reduction and shared prosperity, yet its own citizens endure rising homelessness, suicide rates, drug addiction, and economic inequality. Populist critics of liberal democracy and open markets (Putin, Erdoğan) have overtly exploited these gaps, framing the entire development enterprise as a sham, an insidious form of western neo-imperialism sustained only by creating an illusion of success which in turn only intensifies the cynicism when development reforms inevitably fail to achieve their stated goals. The legitimacy of such reforms is likely to be more secure when there is moral and demonstrated consistency between what their promoters preach and what they themselves actually practice.

Lacking one or more of these forms or sources of process legitimacy, the means of development (i.e., its policies and everyday practices) struggle to become sustainable ends.

3. How competing forms/sources of process legitimacy are reconciled

Process legitimacy comes in many forms, but as noted above, matters can get decidedly complicated and contentious when one group's understanding of what constitutes process legitimacy in any given instance (e.g., how leaders are selected in a highly patriarchal society) varies considerably from that of those with whom they are interacting (say, donors from a Nordic country). This can lead merely to stalemate or confusion (e.g., when the matter is deciding relatively prosaic everyday issues, such as a daily wage rate between strangers) or to more serious misapprehension (e.g., presuming that "property rights" are universally understood); at worst – when the stakes are high (who is the legitimate "owner" or custodian of land), but understandings of process legitimacy between claimants are entirely at cross-purposes (Cronin 1983) – it can lead to violent conflict. As such, a defining aspect of development itself is the extent to which contending forms and sources of process legitimacy (i.e., the foundations on which collective decisions are made and differences are resolved) become increasingly compatible with and acceptable to one another.

Two key steps are required for this to happen. First, an overarching (perhaps interim; see Adler et al. 2009) mechanism acceptable to both parties needs to be established wherein representatives of these parties can forge a path forward that will be regarded as legitimate by the larger membership of both parties; put differently, the task is to identify rules – what might be called "meta-rules"[25] – by which, henceforth, the day-to-day procedures governing their shared interactions will be articulated, enforced, and (when necessary) changed.[26] So understood, development is a process by which a world of idiosyncratic, personalized "deals" governing transactions coheres into a world of unified, broadly endorsed, and transparent "rules."[27] In their own different ways, both De Soto (2000: Chapter 7) and Kleinfeld (2018), for example, explore the dynamics by which informal deals for defining and protecting property rights (De Soto) and establishing order amidst sustained violence (Kleinfeld) can cohere into structured, shared, and legitimate rules enabling greater prosperity and peace.[28] In these cases, one works with what one has, as inherently imperfect as it may be, to build a hybrid system rather than imposing an alien one.

Second, over time, the reconciliation of competing systems of process legitimacy requires not just the forging of new rules *between* groups but the forging of new identities within (and between) groups themselves. An imperative of modernity is the crafting of multiple "sources of the self" (Taylor 1992), in which one assumes "membership" in – and thus takes on a corresponding set of obligations to – an array of different communities (family, faith, ethnicity, occupation, neighborhood, nation), central among them being the state of which one is a citizen.[29] Modernity entails becoming an active member of an ever-larger "community of groups," wherein the moral and cultural integrity of one group is regarded as a complement to (not a substitute for) another. In states such as Papua New Guinea and Afghanistan, seasoned observers routinely lament that it is the taking of this step that has proved most elusive; the state is yet to earn the status and legitimacy needed to secure taxes, and to expect deferment to its rulings, from citizens over and above their more immediately tangible obligations and loyalties to family and tribe.

Both of these steps – the forging of meta-rules to reconcile contending forms of process legitimacy, and the assumption of multiple but coherently integrated identities – are quintessentially "social" tasks. They are enormously difficult to enact and sustain; they require very particular, intentional, frequent, and fraught deliberative work in order to bear the burdens asked of them; measuring progress towards their attainment is deeply problematic (at best); there is only so much that "outsiders" can do to be part of the solution, yet plenty they can do (even or especially with the best of intentions) to be become part of the problem. Even so, creating and sustaining process legitimacy is an abiding development task and its attainment a defining characteristic of what it means for a country to be "developed."

4. Additional evidence

The claims made above have been supported along the way by indicative evidence, to the extent that it is readily available.[30] In this concluding section, I briefly discuss related research that has invoked or explicitly sought to test arguments pertaining to the importance of process legitimacy.

At the global level, a longstanding literature in international relations has sought to identify the sources of legitimacy, some of them historically novel (e.g., international law), upon which multilateral organizations themselves – including, therefore, the World Bank – base their actions (Tallberg and Zürn 2019). A key article by Buchanan and Keohane (2006) distinguishes between "normative" and "sociological" legitimacy, the former being the formal laws giving multilateral agencies mandates for action, the latter comprising the *perceptions* that member states (and, by extension, their citizens) impute to particular measures taken by these agencies. The World Trade Organization (WTO), for example, has authority granted to it by international law and the consent of member governments to oversee trade agreements and mediate specific disputes, which everyone may agree is entirely legitimate; but membership necessarily entails giving consent to a "package deal" of rules, not all of which every member may agree with (e.g., environmental protection), but which they must tolerate in order to get the broader benefits. They may challenge a particular rule they regard as egregious, not merely because it is against their interests to uphold it, but because they perceive the underlying issue to be one over which the WTO has no rightful or legitimate jurisdiction.

When the number or importance of such rules crosses a certain threshold, however, they can be readily leveraged by those seeking to challenge the legitimacy of the entire organization (see also Zürn 2004). As Roger (2020) argues, this dynamic may be one reason why many countries are increasingly preferring "informal" avenues of cross-border dispute resolution – i.e., striking faster and more flexible deals on specific issues with groups such as the G20 and the Financial Stability Board – over the "formal" forums for such resolution within multilateral organizations. Needless to say, such informal organizations lack (by definition) the broader legal powers and legitimacy needed to address truly global problems such as climate change, nuclear proliferation, and pandemics; they may provide expedient, short-term solutions to narrow problems but will likely be insufficiently robust to address the mechanisms enabling and constraining global interaction. Any such mechanisms, however, are merely agreements, signatures on paper; and as events in Ukraine in 2022 painfully remind us, those agreements are only as strong as the enduring legitimacy they are accorded by those that sign them.

Efforts to enhance the quality of governance in "fragile states" are another domain in which the legitimacy of international agencies – their presence, influence, and actions – is surely both important and yet contested. Multilateral agencies such as the World Bank came into existence for the express purpose of "reconstruction and development" (this being the very title of the largest part of the World Bank Group), and they can play a decisive role both in the financial domain (as a lender of last resort and a repository for grants extended to the very poorest countries) and as technical advisors (e.g., providers of expertise on building and consolidating public administration). Recent evaluations of the World Bank's work in fragile/conflict-affected settings (World Bank 2021) suggest that considerable improvements have been made in recent years, and that the Bank can indeed function effectively in such settings, but also that numerous gaps remain regarding its willingness and ability to understand how its own actions engage with prevailing political dynamics: alas, "few sector advisory services and analytics conducted before major warring activities discussed conflict or political economy-related factors. Virtually all sectoral advisory services and analytics conducted before conflict … were not conflict sensitive" (World Bank 2021: ix). Moreover, "[l]ittle is known about how World Bank operations in conflict-affected areas can exacerbate underlying grievances … [T]he percentage of at-risk projects in conflict-affected areas that include mitigation measures remains low and is inconsistent" (xv).

Taking process legitimacy seriously means allocating the time, space, and resources necessary to redress these important concerns, on both intrinsic and instrumental grounds. Doing so is especially important when it comes to changing rules systems themselves (manifest most graphically in attempts to "build the rule of law") and reforming public administration. Why efforts to engage in such tasks so routinely disappoint, and how they might be undertaken in ways that pay close attention to process legitimacy concerns, is the focus of the next chapter.

-3-

Building a Better World: Why Some Problems Are So Much Harder than Others

In the previous chapter, we focused on process legitimacy concerns – specifically, the inadequate attention given to the key issues of *how* development is undertaken. Such oversight, I argue, is one of the key reasons that international development is one of "humanity's biggest challenges." By definition and design, development is about change, yet any change is hard to initiate, hard to sustain, hard to challenge, and often hard to live through. It is harder still when the means by which change is sought is perceived to be alien, unjust, unrealistic, incomprehensible, deceitful, or illegitimate, especially by those who bear its greatest costs with the least resources and fewest alternatives. Relatively few countries have gone from being mostly poor to mostly prosperous without also experiencing a social revolution or major war of one kind or another; even so, it shouldn't take the prospect of societal upheaval for those overseeing the development process to place a strong emphasis on ensuring that citizens experience its many challenges as equitable and legitimate. A commitment to upholding the Golden Rule of "doing as you would be done by" should apply to development decisions and actions as much as it applies everywhere else.[1]

Even if there are bound to be wrenching trade-offs to be made at each point in the development process, the ends (rising prosperity and security) don't axiomatically justify the means (e.g., if this entails destroying forests, suppressing dissent, violating sacred places or practices). Moreover, what counts as an equitable and legitimate development process may not be the same thing for citizens, policymakers, firms, and international agencies, which means it is likely to be contentious. This is another reason – as we also discussed in the previous chapter – why space needs to be created and protected within which resolutions to this contention, and other disputes that inevitably emerge along the way, can be sought. For the extraordinary, historically unprecedented gains in human welfare attained over the last seventy-five years to be extended to all – which is the explicit aspiration of the 193 countries that signed the Sustainable Development Goals in 2015[2] – this "last mile" will likely be the hardest logistically, politically, and ethically (Chandy et al. 2015). It is development's version of the 80/20 Rule: if achieving 80 percent of any task takes 20 percent of the time and effort, and completing the final 20 percent takes 80 percent of the time and effort, then much remains to be done if "sustainable development" really is to be attained by all. Doing so has to be a collective choice to make hard collective decisions about difficult trade-offs – which history suggests is not a task at which humans excel. Put differently, development's proverbial "low-hanging fruit" has mostly been picked; now for the hard part ...

As we noted in the opening chapter, the process of national development, writ large, unfolds across four primary domains – society, politics, the economy, and public administration – as well as the realm of ideas (e.g., how misfortune is explained, how one accords legitimacy to rulers). In the 1950s and 1960s, the stated vision of most countries exiting colonialism or recovering from major wars was not that they would focus on lowering their rate of extreme poverty to below 3 percent but that they would become a vibrant sovereign *nation*, a more prosperous and "modern" version of their current selves, achieved on their own terms but largely via ambitious national planning agencies. For all the numerous challenges realizing this objective entailed – whether from within or because of Cold War politics abroad – the shared conviction was that the attainment of national development would be the means by which countries and their citizens would attain individual human development, not the other way around. In principle, it was (and remains) the task of both "big" and "small" development organizations to facilitate this fourfold transformation in national development and, importantly, to complement its inherent limits: big multi-lateral/bilateral agencies and private foundations providing financial, technical, analytical, and logistical support; small organizations focusing on addressing the specific concerns of particular groups who (by design, default, indifference, or disaster) struggle to meet their basic needs and/or are consistently denied their basic human rights. In practice, however, implementing and assessing every aspect of this transformation has been (and remains) complex; and in our now highly integrated world, both failing or *succeeding* in development ensures that future challenges will only be even more complex.

After further discussion of the social, political, economic, and administrative aspects of national development (and the ideas associated with them), the rest of this chapter and the next explore the specific ways in which designing, prioritizing, implementing, and assessing efforts to bring about change have proven to be such a vexing challenge – especially when it comes to "building the rule of law" and promoting greater social inclusion.

National development as a fourfold transformation[3]

As we noted in Chapter 1, when most people speak of countries that have become "developed" they are referring, implicitly or explicitly, to a cumulative historical process whereby economies grow through enhanced productivity,[4] prevailing political systems represent the aggregate preferences of citizens,[5] rights and opportunities are extended to all social groups,[6] and public organizations function according to meritocratic standards and professional norms (thereby becoming capable of administering ever-larger numbers of more technically and logistically complex tasks).[7] In and through such processes, a given country undergoes a fourfold transformation in its functional capacity to manage its economy, polity, society, and public administration, becoming, in time, "developed" (see Figure 3.1). When in everyday speech people say that France – as an ontologically distinct category and not merely as an aggregation of the people living in France – is "more developed" than Congo, or that Denmark is more developed than Nepal, they mean, inter alia, that France has undergone more of this fourfold functional transformation than the Congo, and Denmark more than Nepal.

As Figure 3.1 imperfectly shows, an additional feature of the development process is that it separates the four realms of society, polity, economy, and public administration into discrete entities, requiring people to move between qualitatively different roles as (say) family member, citizen, employee, and taxpayer. This was the essence of Karl Polanyi's (1944) classis thesis on the "great transformation," in which he argued that, as a result of the development process, "the economy" became increasingly dis-embedded from "society" and both thereby became subject to different logics, rules, expectations, obligations, and power relations. In those countries or communities at the center of Figure 3.1, these four realms remain essentially one and the same: religious, political, judicial, commercial, and civic leadership, for example, is exercised as (and by) a single entity. A defining feature of modernity, by contrast, is the *separation* of church and state, the *separation* of executive, judicial, and legislative powers, of science and religion, of media and state (a "free press"), and of knowledge into discrete professional "disciplines," etc. This is a process that, historically, has often been accompanied by great conflict as shifts transpire across identities, roles, responsibilities, mandates, and sources of wealth, status, and power. To be in the development business is to be in the business of generating new sources and forms of contention.

The central premise of the development enterprise is that today's "less" developed countries can, should, and eventually

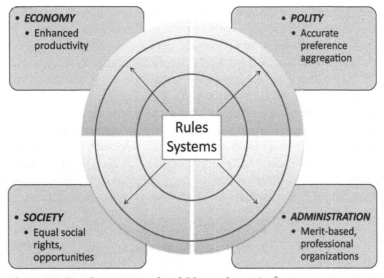

Figure 3.1 Development as a fourfold transformation[8]
Source: Author's adaptation from Pritchett, Woolcock, and Andrews (2013)

will undergo their own fourfold transformation and thereby become "more" developed. The task of the development project and its promoters (domestic and foreign) is to accelerate this transformation, to speed up a process that, left to its own devices, would occur, but too slowly or haphazardly, thereby increasing global inequalities. "Big development" agencies are structured on the premise that how these transformations unfold is known (or at least knowable) – that is, they believe, though they may not explicitly articulate it in such terms, that there is a common underlying structure characterizing these transformations, and that as such their primary objective should be to facilitate (via the deployment of their resources and staff through instruments known as "projects") this ongoing transformational process, the better to bring it about in a faster and more equitable manner. As befits a system believed to have oversight over a common underlying structure, professional skills acquired in one development sector and setting (e.g., agricultural extension in Pakistan) are regarded as being readily transferable to another (e.g., social development in Egypt). The common, if completely hidden, foundation for big development agencies, agents, and agendas is modernization, which, for lack of any broadly credible alternative, everyone still relies on as bedrock.

Over the past five decades, however, a fundamental paradox has emerged at the heart of development theory and practice. The paradox is that *everyone and no one believes in modernization*. If everybody (explicitly or implicitly) still believes that development entails the modernization of economic, political, social, and administrative life, no one (for all intents and purposes) now overtly champions modernization *theory*.[9] It was not always thus; what gave modernization theory such widespread potency in its prime in the 1950s and 1960s was that both the political right and the political left believed that history was unfolding according to some inevitable Hegelian teleology, and that the culmination of this process – capitalism (for the right) or communism (for the left) – would be a convergence of institutional forms.[10] Thus the fastest and most expedient route to modernity was to adopt the "forms" of those countries further along this path, and to do so via a "great push."

But, if asked, few contemporary development practitioners would explicitly espouse this view. Development discourse is now replete with anti-modernization-theory aphorisms: "one size doesn't fit all," "there are no silver bullets," "context matters," etc. Most development professionals are extraordinarily well traveled and are acutely conscious of, and actively celebrate, cultural difference. Nearly all would agree that low-income countries "should be in the driver's seat" when it comes to determining the content, direction, and speed of their development policies, and thereby (implicitly) reject modernization theory.

Rejection of modernization theory in principle, however, has not dislodged modernization theory (or a latter-day version thereof) in practice, greatly undermining the coherence of efforts to enhance implementation effectiveness. This has created a situation in which the *idea* of development (as a fourfold modernization process of economy, polity, society, and administration) and the *business* of development (as a loosely linked movement/industry structured to disseminate

standardized solutions) are conjointly underpinned by a
theory of change that conspires against serious engagement
with complex implementation issues. This theory of change
can be fairly characterized as "accelerated modernization
via transplanted best practice." In other words, the abiding
theory of change that underpins the actions of most "national
development" ministries and "big development" agencies is
one that seeks to modernize institutions by intensifying a
process of reform via the importing of methods and designs
deemed effective elsewhere. Such an approach, it should be
acknowledged, can be entirely appropriate for those development problems that do indeed have a universal technical
solution, where there genuinely is no need to reinvent the
wheel. Effective low-cost vaccines should of course be made
available to all; there are only so many tools for combating
hyperinflation. For many central aspects of political, administrative, and legal reform, however, and for the delivery of
key public services – especially health, justice, and education,
which require enormous numbers of discretionary face-to-
face transactions (Pritchett and Woolcock 2004) – reform
via cut-and-paste borrowings from a foreign setting is no
reform at all. In such instances, much of the wheel must be
reinvented, each and every time, to imbue it with local content
and legitimacy. For big development agencies, however,
organizational imperatives overwhelmingly favor tackling
problems, or those aspects of problems, that lend themselves
to technical, universal answers.

Nowhere in development is this dynamic on more graphic
and consequential display than in efforts to "build the rule of
law." A common element across all four domains discussed
above is that they function on the basis of rules systems of
one kind or another, these rules systems themselves under-
going fundamental changes during the development process.
Indeed, a broad measure of "development," as we noted
in previous chapters, is the extent to which a world replete
with informal idiosyncratic deals becomes one upheld and
enforced by uniform, codified laws, this transformation being
made possible and given coherence by an overarching system
called "the rule of law" (Tamanaha 2004; Bingham 2010;

Pirie 2021). Yet despite its widely endorsed importance, there is surely no sector in development where the gap between high shared aspiration and consistently low performance is wider, where expectations and lived experience are so far apart. Why is this?

Building the rule of law: why such a long and "fragile path of progress"?[11]

Assessing efforts to build or reform the rule of law in developing countries – that is, the relationship between the rule of law as a historical-political ideal and the policies and programs that might instantiate it – has a history spanning almost five decades, dating back to the foundational article of Trubek and Galanter (1974). When observing the veritable cottage industry that has arisen over this time lamenting the world's inability to build the rule of law,[12] it is conspicuous that all contributors, without fail, point to – and attempt to resolve – deep first-order conceptual or methodological faults. There is much marshy ground in the field, and what small islands there are on which to build alternatives remain fragile and unmoored. For example, as a seminal article on rule-of-law reform argues, *all* of the literature to date is "ultimately unhelpful" because of a deep foundational failing, namely "the absence of a more careful theoretical account of how law functions to achieve legal order in a way that is responsive to policy goals" (Hadfield and Weingast 2014: 22). In other words, the link between the ideal and its instantiation fails because we lack an adequate applied theory to link them, despite many decades of work on the subject.

This begs the question of why such critiques persist. Why does the field of rule-of-law reform seemingly remain impervious to these insights? Indeed, what work might such critiques actually do to *sustain* the "old" and "failed" ways of doing business, or to push policy and programming in a direction that might always already be unsuccessful (whatever such an evaluative judgment might mean)? Rather than develop a general theory of the rule of law, or of its relationship to institutional change, it is more fruitful to articulate an applied theory of the rule of law as an artefact within the field of development policymaking, programming, and practice. This will, of course, be heavily influenced by the literature on the rule of law already canvassed elsewhere, but it is also framed and directed by the literature on the practice of development. Any critical moves in the field of rule-of-law reform, however, are plagued by foundational challenges with respect to scope and content. If the rule of law is "essentially contested" (Waldron 2002), if we indeed "know how to do a lot of things, but deep down we don't really know what we are doing" (Carothers 2006: 15), we cannot draw neat lines around our field (Desai 2014) – even though we might believe that there is some determinate content to the rule of law itself (Krygier 2015). Indeed, some question whether or not rule-of-law reform is indeed a bona fide "field" in the absence of "a well-grounded rationale, a clear understanding of the essential problem, a proven analytic method, and an understanding of results achieved" (Carothers 2006: 28).[13]

As a result, many critiques of the rule of law are founded on a story of fundamental *deficiency* that inevitably results from – and is easy to find in a field structured around – a concept that eludes definitional consensus. The primary modality of such critiques is "taking into account": they require us (1) to generate more precise definitions of the rule of law by taking into account insights from conceptual, analytical/discursive and practical thinking;[14] (2) to consult other genres of literature that might tell us more about the rule of law (Comaroff and Comaroff 2004; Krygier 2012); and (3) to engage with stories about the structures and individual actors who "build" or "reform" it in particular contexts (Golub 2003; Isser 2011; Desai and Woolcock 2015). Efforts to coalesce and move forwards, then, are structurally impeded by a combination of repeated first-order questioning and an inadequate consensus about conceptual foundations.

Such critiques can assert that they have a theory of application when they actually provide theory or applied theory (and vice versa). This helps us unpick how knowledge claims within the field inhibit the production of that missing "bridge." In their review, Hadfield and Weingast presume to offer the missing microfoundational account of the rule of law needed in order to rectify the "gaps" that have led to "two decades of largely failed efforts to build the rule of law in poor and transition countries and continuing struggles to build international legal order" (2014: 21). Indeed, they present their practical bona fides by including a subsection on "applied theory" of the rule of law (a critique of the definitions used by the World Bank, the World Justice Project, and others), enabling them to conclude that there are "several problems with the applied world of rule-of-law assistance, including its tendency to use the concept as a cover for projects to achieve particular political goals or establish specific institutions" (2014: 37). Yet their new institutionalist account is highly limited on the applied side. It is open to critiques from applied theory – for the absence of any recursive relationship between the production of subjectivity (that is, a way of producing the subject as someone who makes meaning of the world) and the classifications (i.e., legal/illegal) emanating from the legal institution, along with the absence of power more generally from their account. And it is certainly lacking in a theory of application. In fact, Hadfield and Weingast suggest as much: "We do not yet have an answer to the question of how to build legal order in places in which it does not currently exist" (2014: 23).

The task of constructing an "applied theory of application" of the rule of law thus requires acknowledging (and accommodating, operationally) the pervasive tension between determining and un-determining action, and allowing space for the particular intrinsic value of law. Such an approach requires a different modality of engagement with rule-of-law reform, a modality we might call a "new experimentalism," which centers on solving problems (not selling predetermined solutions), and on understanding the context-specific ways in which multiple rules systems,[15] many of them informal, interact at the local level, and the political economy dynamics shaping their engagement with the state. This approach, manifest in the World Bank's Justice for the

Poor program (2002–15) (see Box 3.1), informed subsequent efforts that became the broader Building State Capability program based at Harvard Kennedy School (Andrews et al. 2017).[16] Both programs were/are premised on engaging with development problems that are essentially socially contested and yet have to instantiate real power and authority (public administration, governance) – which is fundamental to any particularities of law.

These innovative efforts to engage with justice reform "from below," alongside numerous parallel initiatives in the "small development" (research and advocacy) space, such as the World Justice Project[17] and Namati,[18] contributed to "justice" being included as one of the Sustainable Development Goals – as part of goal #16, which calls for providing "access to justice for all."[19] They are efforts grounded in attempts to instantiate an alternative ontological understanding of what law "is" and, on that basis, engage with its multiple forms and sources within ongoing context-specific development processes. Even when housed inside the World Bank, however, initiatives such as Justice for the Poor are relatively marginal, seeking to influence at scale rather than operate at scale – and for which history will be the best judge of their effectiveness. Even so, they show that space can be created and protected within "big" agencies for "doing development differently," and that serious efforts can be made to apprehend, engage with, and assess non-technical aspects of the change process. In this sense, lessons from initiatives like Justice for the Poor become instructive for a host of other sectors replete with their own non-technical (and inherently contested) characteristics.

Beyond the justice sector, many key development problems, it turns out, are not technical but instead adaptive (Honig 2018). Such problems may require lots of people to interact for long periods of time (e.g., classroom teaching), the "right" response to them is likely to be largely unknown at the outset (e.g., how to consolidate a peace agreement), they may be subject to organized resistance (e.g., from the military, unions, opposition parties), be decidedly unglamorous (e.g., enforcing order in remote communities), and take a dozen

Box 3.1 The World Bank's Justice for the Poor program, 2002–2015

A key consideration in the implementation of Justice for the Poor (J4P) was to set aside preconceived notions about the efficacy of particular law, justice, and security institutions and instead focus on problems of injustice as experienced by the "users," rather than just the "providers," of prevailing justice systems. Early country engagements supported by J4P after 2008 in Timor-Leste and Melanesia confirmed a program focus on contests in three thematic areas – social order, land/natural resources, and the distribution of public rents/wealth – reflecting the experience that this was where conflict-driving social contests were most pronounced, and where the risks of regulatory failure were greatest for growth, equality, and security. These engagements highlighted that a focus on "best practice" reforms to formal state systems could potentially do harm to vital governance capabilities – both within the state and in the wider non-state domains – needed to handle contests and disputes and to produce justice and security.

Responding to this concern reinforced J4P's design commitment to invest in sustained, locally grounded field research. It was obviously important to distinguish potentially "good," socially generative contests from those that the World Development Report 2006 on equity (World Bank 2005) had labelled "inequality traps," which were thus detrimental to social order, political stability, and economic transformation. But the available techniques and practices used by donors to engage in these contexts were ill-suited. Two decades of donor "good governance" engagements had produced a raft of metrics and templates to measure the gaps between the governance reforms prescribed and formal appearances, but they were not well suited to understanding how problems were perceived and handled locally; that is, to understanding governance in practice.

Thus, the program developed a distinctive "cascade" of questions through which it aimed to understand the nature of the problems being experienced by everyday people, how people were currently being governed, and with what consequences for women and vulnerable sectors. Analysis of the political economy underlying these contests enabled program staff and their counterparts to identify the conditions under which external interventions are likely to be positively generative or to risk doing harm. How these analytic questions were framed and the interventions they gave rise to varied with country, team, thematic area, and throughout the life of the program. The concepts and efforts to put them into practice ranged from pre-2008 activities (in Kenya, Cambodia, Indonesia) through to 2016, where the focus in particular was on countries in the western Pacific (Timor-Leste, Papua New Guinea, Solomon Islands, and Vanuatu). These efforts were bookended by substantive contributions to three influential World Development Reports: on equity (World Bank 2005), conflict and security (World Bank 2011), and governance (World Bank 2017a).

Source: World Bank (2018a); see also Sage et al. (2010) and https://www.worldbank.org/en/topic/governance/brief/justice-for-the-poor

years or more to achieve, thus needing to cross several electoral cycles (e.g., upgrading public financial management systems). Building a better world thus requires attending to both the technical and the adaptive tasks, because everything depends on everything else. Even if individuals can only work on a small slice of a given problem in a particular place, having a broader appreciation of the complexities of the development process gives people an acute awareness that they can do what they do because others (mostly unknown to them) are doing what they do, probably in obscurity and often under considerable duress. It is especially incumbent upon leaders to recognize that the success of large complex efforts depends on protecting the space in which both technical and adaptive development challenges are being addressed, often in ways requiring entirely different skillsets, mindsets, theories, instruments, evidence, and measures of success.

The importance of enhancing capability for policy implementation in general, and for responding to the distinctive challenges that different *kinds* of development problems pose to both implementers and evaluators, has a host of broader implications for policymakers, practitioners, researchers, and the givers and receivers of development assistance. We consider some of these implications in the next section.

If quality of implementation matters, what underlying principles might enhance it?[20]

Learning that effective implementation matters for attaining development outcomes is hardly revolutionary. Or is it? One struggles to name even three development books that focus on this issue, yet there are literally hundreds on "politics" or "policy." Which is to say, most of the intellectual bandwidth allocated to explaining development outcomes is concerned with power, incentives, design, and resources. All of these issues are clearly important, but when our gaze does turn to implementation issues the associated discourse mostly centers on "capacity building," which translates into interventions or recommendations offering a standard mix of enhancing training sessions, consulting (foreign) experts, adopting new technology, and transferring "best practices." As noted above, these too have their place, especially when the core problem is (or key components of a broader problem are) essentially technical. But as the findings on implementation dynamics from recent research makes clear, non-technical problems – i.e., problems characterized by (a) numerous discretionary social interactions (e.g., teaching, social work, curative care)[21] and (b) inherent ambivalence ex ante as to what constitutes the optimal solution – usually require non-technical (or "adaptive") solutions. Such solutions are deeply idiosyncratic, context-specific, teamwork-dependent, and need to be forged iteratively in situ.[22] As such, they transfer poorly from one group or place to another; one cannot assume they are readily scale-able; and their associated metrics (e.g., of "success") are likely to be contested, relatively opaque, and unstable over time. Yet adaptive problems infuse many key sectors in development (education, health, justice), and failure to address them on their own terms is one of the primary reasons why development efforts underperform (Pritchett and Woolcock 2004).[23]

If implementation matters to achieving development outcomes in general, and if responding effectively to "adaptive" problems during the implementation process matters in particular, then I argue that three key constituent principles need to be taken seriously by those designing such interventions, and especially those assessing and interpreting assessments of their effectiveness.

1. Uphold process legitimacy

As we noted in the previous chapter, *how* difficult/contentious outcomes are reached – e.g., elections, judicial rulings, inequalities – has enormous bearing on their legitimacy, and thus the extent to which they are accepted, especially by those who would have strongly preferred a different outcome. Political parties that lose close elections accept this outcome if they believe the votes were cast and counted impartially; citizens tolerate higher levels of inequality to the extent that the wealthy are perceived as having gained their riches by diligence, innovation, and prudence (not theft, deception, or corruption).[24] This everyday reality is vastly underappreciated by development agencies and economics more generally, but findings from behavioral economics, insights from development practitioners, and longstanding results from social psychology are steadily giving it more traction.

Development, by definition, is about social change, but change is always hard; even if eventual outcomes are net positive in terms of human welfare, many people are likely to be worse off than before (at least in the short run), and the journey to a net positive destination may entail weathering genuine hardship for an extended period of time (e.g., migration to cities, loss of ancestral land, shifts in identity and livelihood). This matters enormously for development agencies and governments alike, because *how* such difficult change is promoted – e.g., "building the rule of law," modernizing the public sector, diversifying employment, expanding health and education – will play a large role in shaping its legitimacy and thus the willingness of citizens to embrace the uncertain social challenges accompanying it. How such legitimacy is secured and sustained is likely to be deeply context-specific, varying considerably between and within countries. Even professional "best practices" (fiscal rules, meritocratic hiring) and scientifically verified "solutions" (immunizations, fertilizers) must earn local legitimacy and credibility before they will be embraced, at scale; creating public spaces within which such practices and solutions can be adapted to the local context, and/or be deployed to find better ones, is central to establishing their legitimacy and thus their (eventual, potential) effectiveness.

2. Forge an explicit theory of change against which evidence is interpreted

The empirical basis on which decisions pertaining to an intervention's effectiveness are made requires, of necessity, dialogue with a corresponding theory of change – that is, a formalized articulation of the sequenced mechanisms by which the provision of particular inputs will yield a desired outcome, *assessed against the timeframe and trajectory over which it can reasonably be expected to be apparent.* As with process legitimacy concerns, the importance of this latter aspect is also vastly underappreciated: one cannot determine whether one's efforts at implementing a given development intervention are "working" or not without an informed sense of when and how such a conclusion can be drawn. What should one conclude, for example, if, after two years of honest efforts at empowering marginalized communities, there has been no apparent "impact," as discerned by a "rigorous" methodology? Taken at face value, one might conclude that the intervention has "failed." But what if experiences elsewhere suggest that it takes at least five years for "results" with such interventions to be observed? Despite the apparent failure after two years, should one just hang in there and wait for vindication when positive outcomes (hopefully) materialize in five years, or is this initial result actually an indication that, *in this case*, further effort is futile and should be abandoned? Rigorous methodology alone cannot solve these types of problems; rigorous-enough methodology in conversation with an articulated theory of change stands a slightly better chance.[25]

Most people, or at least most non-researchers, regard "theory" as a rather pejorative term – something merely speculative, abstract, or the opposite of useful and useable. Theory can surely be all those things, but it is especially important when trying to make sense of deeply complex phenomena, and when trying to function in novel contexts; as smiling academics sometimes like to say, "There's nothing more practical than a good theory." I guess I'm one of those people, so for present purposes I want to make the case for deploying theory in a very specific way; namely, assessing performance data against a set of reasoned expectations about what can be expected of an intervention and by when, in a particular setting.

For those assessing interventions of any kind, one of the most commonly invoked concepts is the "counterfactual," or what would have otherwise happened to recipients of a program or policy in the absence of that intervention. The theory behind the concept of a counterfactual draws on a longstanding scientific (Cartesian) idea that the world largely functions like a machine, and that the task of analysts is to identify both whether and how the different "parts" of the machine are integrated. Causality is thus determined by holding constant all but one of the most salient aspects of the machine and comparing it to an identical machine operating under the same conditions:[26] if there are differences in the respective machines' performance, it can be causally attributed to the 'treatment variable' (i.e., the variable present in one set of circumstances but not the other).

Stressing the "social" aspects of social science, however, requires recognizing that all sorts of known and unknown factors can routinely and ubiquitously interfere with the purity of this model, leaving researchers to impose stringent restrictions to ensure that as many of these factors as possible are indeed "controlled for." In its purest form, researchers have long prized the randomized controlled trial (RCT) as the ideal, since it enables factors pertaining to structure (e.g., demographic and geographic characteristics), selection (psychological and social issues shaping who joins and stays in a program), and potential researcher bias (treating participants and non-participants differently) to be minimized. For many vital questions in the world, such as discerning the effectiveness of new medicines, this is the "gold standard" approach – i.e., the way we want and expect such research to be conducted. One would not ingest a new medicine, for example, unless its efficacy had been verified by such an approach.

But in most of social science, as philosopher Nancy Cartwright (2007) has famously written, "there is no gold standard."[27] Put differently, the number of important problems in the universe of social science that can actually be assessed this way – logistically, ethically, politically, substantively – is surely very small; and since important social problems rarely map neatly onto a singular methodology, the optimal strategy is to have access to a range of different approaches that can be called upon as required (Woolcock 2019a). In the matter of assessing the efficacy of complex interventions (as defined above), one can (and should) retain the *principle* of thinking in terms of counterfactuals while in practice recognizing that they are nearly always unobservable, politically difficult, and ethically vexing, and thus that creative "second-best" efforts will be needed to establish them. (In the most complex interventions of all there is, by definition, no counterfactual since each episode is uniquely distinctive and unrepeatable.)

For present purposes, however, I want to stress the importance for evaluators of taking time seriously – of recognizing that the empirical journey of an intervention from "baseline" to "follow-up" is rarely straight (Woolcock

2009), even though it is routinely presumed to be so. Once one concedes that the trajectory of change in complex development interventions is highly likely to be both non-linear and non-uniform, then even at face value one must recognize that *when* an evaluation is conducted matters enormously. It is largely by default that follow-up evaluations in development are conducted after three to five years, because this happens to be the typical administrative/political "life" of such projects. But to expect a positive "result" within such a timeframe requires a theory of change articulating why it is reasonable for an "effect" to be detectable within such a timeframe. Three years may well be a reasonable period within which to expect infrastructure and energy projects to yield positive impacts, but history suggests a rather different timeframe and trajectory for, say, "building the rule of law," effecting public sector reform, or promoting gender equality. By analogy, even the most casual gardener does not expect the seeds of sunflowers and oak trees to show similar "results" six months after planting, because, implicitly, the gardener assesses progress against reasoned expectations: sunflowers grow remarkably fast and oak trees grow remarkably slowly. Likewise, evidence from evaluations of development interventions should be assessed against their own articulated theory of change; without this, all manner of false inferences about the effectiveness of implementation effects are likely to be drawn (Woolcock 2019a).

3. Map, explore, and explain outcome variation

A defining characteristic of even well-designed and faithfully implemented complex interventions is that they will have high outcome variation.[28] Consider health and education for example: in addition to having clear technical components their effective delivery also entails giving close attention to social (non-technical) processes. Stopping contagious diseases (e.g., Ebola) requires changing behavior among entire populations, while preparing a young adult for an entry-level job in the modern global economy requires at least 12,000 hours of classroom instruction.[29] As the recent

World Development Report on learning amply demonstrated (World Bank 2018b), most countries have "sound policies" pertaining to the provision of universal primary education, but there is enormous variation, especially among and within low-income countries, in how such policies are implemented with regard to achieving student learning (as opposed to merely school attendance). A relatively poor country such as Vietnam, for example, has managed to design and implement an education system that delivers learning outcomes commensurate with those of OECD countries, while some middle-income countries can place students in schools for ten years yet fail to teach half of them how to do basic tasks such as double-digit subtraction or reading a newspaper headline. Identifying and explaining such variation is both an important research task and a valuable source of insight into how, why, and for whom effective implementation happens (or not).

In health, recent research (Sterck et al. 2018) strongly suggests that, beyond roughly a national per capita income level of $10,000, there is relatively little variation in how effectively countries respond to both communicable and non-communicable diseases (as measured by the number of "disability-adjusted life years" (DALYs) lost as a result of these diseases). However, in countries with per capita incomes below $10,000 there is especially wide variation in how they address communicable diseases – i.e., those medical conditions spread through direct human interaction. A key reason for this variation, I suggest, is that responding to communicable diseases is a different and more complex kind of implementation challenge than responding to medical conditions that do not entail human interaction (such as physical injury or cancer), because it requires changing people's behavior, and potentially their intimate behavior, which is extraordinarily difficult for any single "policy" to do. This same logic, however, suggests that there is also likely to be considerable within-country variation in how poor countries respond to communicable diseases. The potential for such variation is apparent in even the most routine aspects of medical care which also entail shifting human behavior: drawing on houschold surveys conducted in several countries in the Middle East and North Africa, where policies (of all kinds) are strongly set at the national level, Brixi et al. (2015) show that there is wide variation all the way down to the district level in seemingly elementary, non-controversial behaviors such as showing up for work.[30]

Two (unresolvable?) conundrums

Even if evaluators of implementation efforts dutifully honor these three principles, I think there nonetheless remain issues that are unsolvable within the logics by which public policy and programmatic decisions are made; I shall call them conundrums. Importantly, I do not regard such conundrums as epistemological "weaknesses" that, one day soon, will be solved by diligent researchers as they further refine their methodological tools; rather, such issues can only be resolved deliberatively, collectively, and inclusively – which is to say, through some local-level version of democratic politics (Rao 2019). Indeed, we should not want these conundrums declared "solved" or even "solvable" in a technical sense, because they define the bounded space within which reasoned differences about the contested means and ends of development are negotiated. There is no right answer to such problems, in the same way there isn't a right answer to the optimal location of the church–state boundary or the optimal level or form of taxation: one can make an empirical case for *an* answer in a particular context, but under different reasonable assumptions different reasonable people can reach rather different reasonable conclusions. Which of these "reasonable" options prevails at a particular time and place is optimally determined by political consent; this in turn requires establishing robust institutional processes able to "contain" (and, as necessary, constrain) the inherently contested claims and counterclaims made by different groups, and thereby publicly confer legitimacy on the outcome(s).[31]

Doubtless there are many such conundrums in development, but here I focus on just two.

1. Discerning when to stay the course, make adjustments, or concede defeat

I argued above that making calls on the effectiveness of development interventions requires evidence grounded in a sound methodology (a plausible counterfactual) assessed in the light of a theory of change: that is, of the mechanisms by which inputs connect to outcomes, in dialogue with reasoned expectations about what should be achieved by when (a plausible "counter-temporal," as it were). A conundrum emerges, however, when the theory of change, so understood, just cannot be clearly specified, when time horizons are existentially short (e.g., at the height of a political campaign or a public health emergency) or necessarily long, or when groups undertake development activities in accordance with "higher" values – e.g., political, professional, religious, cultural, familial – that are not subject, perhaps rightly, to empirical refutation.[32]

Let me give some specific examples. Even if all the major participants agree on the importance of ending a civil war, the task of actually achieving and sustaining it will entail preparing plans that, at the outset, can largely be expressed only in terms of aspiration, as well as making subsequent decisions that rely heavily on hard-won experience, real-time learning, and political expedience in response to deeply contingent events. After thousands of years of such wars, there just is not, and never will be, a clear "theory" or "evidence base" deftly spelling out what should be done by whom, on what basis over what timeframe; it's a defining reason (among many) why ending war is so wrenchingly difficult.[33] Certainly one can learn from "successful" experiences elsewhere, and at the extremes it is doubtless possible to make demonstrably "good" and "bad" decisions, but for modal cases in which the stakes are so high, the "lessons" so vexing,[34] the context(s) so fluid, and the theory–evidence connection so (inherently) thin, there cannot be a firm foundation on which to act. Reasoned decisions must still be made, to be sure, but in the end it is the task of senior leaders to make judgment calls and live with the consequences, come what may. Less dramatically, I suspect many of the vexing discussions seeking to discern the determinants of "what works" in fragile states are instances of this conundrum.

A more prosaic example is decisions based on implicit deference to professional norms. If someone were to somehow conduct a rigorous study of high-level conferences and show that the costs of such gatherings simply far outweighed the benefits, would a decision be made to henceforth cease holding such gatherings? No, of course not, because professionals participate in such conferences because that's what such people do; our actions in this instance (and many others) are made independently of what "the evidence" says (or might say) about their "effectiveness." In these types of situations, normal social science will have little traction in terms of guiding decisions as to whether one should persist with a given course of action, make changes, or give up. Similarly, for many advocacy NGOs, partisan think-tanks, and faith-based organizations doing development work, both the goals they pursue and the strategies by which they seek to realize them are grounded in the specific logics that define their "epistemic community" – that is, the basis on which what counts as a question and what counts as an answer is determined, which often transcends the contours of "normal social science."

Consider a different example. If, during an election season, someone commits to a political party because of a deeply felt affinity with its values and goals, they may continue to donate time and money to its cause when all "the evidence" suggests the campaign is doomed. If the evidence turns out to be flawed, and the party goes on to win the election, it may well have been the actions of those campaigners who persisted nonetheless that ultimately brought victory; such tales then become the inspiring narratives that will be summoned when future efforts seem futile, even as failing to heed subsequently vindicated evidence can lead to calamitous results (e.g., those in the path of a Category 5 hurricane who decide to stay put). I stress again how normal and ubiquitous such decisions are; indeed, I strongly suspect that a world in which *all* decisions were made in accordance with science and social science would be one that is decidedly less interesting and more fraught.[35] So understood, this conundrum suggests that development administrators need an overarching framework for deciding which kinds of problems will be addressed in which kinds of ways. However, since the essentially contested nature of any such framework would render it unworkable, the conundrum endures: in the most difficult circumstances, whether in life (getting married, raising children) or in development practice (empowering marginalized groups), deciding when to persist, when to adjust, and when to cut one's losses can only ever be partially informed by "the evidence."

2. Discerning when to prioritize instrumental vs intrinsic criteria

A related but narrower conundrum is when to prioritize either instrumental or intrinsic criteria when responding to key questions in development – questions that may initially seem empirical and thus answerable on the basis of "the evidence" but which upon closer inspection are more complicated. This conundrum becomes apparent when one seeks to provide general advice to everyday citizens or to those seeking a career in international development about how best to "reduce global poverty" or "make a difference in the world." Given finite resources, are optimal outcomes achieved by seeking broad-but-slow improvements in institutions and systems or by applying "proven" interventions to specific poor/marginalized people? Is it better to promote good things (schools, hospitals, roads) or to stop bad things (violence, exploitation, discrimination)? Should one give money to existing aid organizations (and trust their "development professionals") or work directly with poor communities (e.g., volunteering at a homeless shelter or going on a short-term visit to construct a school in a poor country)? In an interconnected world, should concerned global citizens focus on influencing the actions of rich countries (e.g., redressing their outsized role in climate change, reducing their agricultural subsidies) or those of poor countries (e.g., reducing "corruption," promoting inclusive growth)?

I am often asked variations on these questions, and the answers to them matter; I do my best to provide a reasoned response (see this book's Epilogue!). For these types of questions, however, providing "evidence-based" answers is necessary but insufficient; there isn't a "right" answer, because the asker's talents, values, level of commitment, opportunity to contribute, and their very definition of "development" shapes what will count as an answer. For these big-picture questions, there is rarely a direct match between "what the evidence says" and what any particular individual concerned about development issues might "do" with it. In the twenty-first century, the development ecosystem has become a veritable hyperspace, with an extraordinary variety of actors, instruments, financing mechanisms, evaluation imperatives, and accountability structures operating in every conceivable sector at scales ranging from individual families and national ministries to regional associations[36] and global agencies. Even so, the basic logics of national, big, and small development (as discussed in Chapter 1) endure, as does the division of labor between them. Staff at multi-lateral agencies explaining how Vietnam achieved perhaps the fastest sustained period of poverty reduction in history (World Bank 2018b) will note that this was not the result of implementing thousands of "proven" small-scale initiatives, while NGO staff can rightly point to "rigorous evidence" demonstrating that, controlling for key factors, certain child sponsorship programs in developing countries clearly enhance the welfare and lifetime earnings opportunities of participants (Wydick et al. 2013).

Importantly, both of these accounts can be fully correct and yet provide no neat answer to those wanting to know which approach to poverty reduction is "best." If the accurate response to such questions is "it depends," then I think it is helpful to reply that a key factor on which an answer depends is powerfully shaped by one's (often implicit) understanding of what development is and, accordingly, where one's particular talents or resources best fit within that understanding. I like to think that I've found my niche after a quarter century of engagement with the development space, but during that time I've been privileged to meet with people operating at all points within it, and it's hard not to conclude that it is the collective efforts of all these people that matters more than the singular "effectiveness" of a particular instrument, method, organization, or individual.

Hence the conundrum, and hence, in part, the non-resolvability of the virtues/vices/limits of singular approaches unless one has (a) a broader encompassing theory (or "map") in which one can locate such differences and the (likely very limited) space in which the deployment of any given singular approach makes sense; and (b) a corresponding framework for discerning when one's efforts should be assessed against instrumental (efficiency/effectiveness) criteria versus intrinsic (fidelity to reasoned values) criteria. In effect, then, the conundrum turns on how, where, and with whom one seeks to make a difference in the world; and reasonable people can choose (and/or be called upon) to enter development via the "national," "big," or "small" door, even as they should retain an abiding sense that everyone needs to keep learning,[37] everyone needs a basis for discerning the wisdom/folly of their actions, and everyone needs to be a faithful steward of the resources and skills entrusted to them.

Conclusion

A policy is only as good as its implementation. Forging and adopting sound policy in the technical sense is of course preferable to its opposite, but too often development professionals go little further: we seek to explore the "policy implications" of our analytical work and hope it will influence "policymakers," but far less frequently do we take the next step and ask whether the prevailing administrative apparatus charged with delivering this "policy" (e.g., promoting foreign investment, regulating firms, providing clean water) can actually do so. Efforts such as those embodied in the work of Princeton University's Innovations for Successful Societies[38] are one practical way in which development practitioners and researchers can focus their energies on gaining a better understanding of the conditions under which more effective implementation happens (see also McDonnell 2020).

Realizing our respective organizations' corporate objectives, and (more importantly) helping our national development counterparts to realize theirs, will entail not only the adoption of better policies, continuing to secure adequate resources, and negotiating vexing political constraints, but also giving vastly more focused attention to *how* to build implementation capability. Acquiring more and better evidence must necessarily be part of this process, but evidence alone does not yield self-evident conclusions and implications (Bridges and Woolcock 2022): these require good theory, which in turn requires forging a conversation between the evidence and our articulated expectations of the specific mechanisms that will yield desired outcomes within a reasoned timeframe following a particular trajectory. Even when all these aspects are carefully attended to, however, there will remain in development crucial questions and decisions whose resolution defies the contours of normal social science; therein lie vexing conundrums. Respecting these limits, and the decisions of those with greater hard-won experience or who have been elected/nominated to make precisely such difficult decisions, is perhaps itself a characteristic of the effective researcher, policymaker, and practitioner.

Our prevailing architecture for "doing development" was not, and is not, designed to address such concerns. These types of challenges will be even more daunting in the coming years because development *success* (let alone failure) will entail implementing tasks that are increasingly complex at a time when – as we noted in Chapter 1 – current evidence suggests that the capability of today's policy implementation systems in development countries is mostly declining. Moreover, having set expectations so high with the ratification of the Sustainable Development Goals, there is a strong likelihood of a widening gap between these lofty expectations and the reality of everyday experience, a gap which historically has been politically volatile. Moreover, in key domains such as "building the rule of law" – a space that is central to ensuring that contention is addressed in ways broadly perceived to be legitimate, and that inherently disruptive transitions across society, the economy, politics, and public administration have avenues for peaceful redress – the track record of accomplishment to date is especially concerning.

What kinds of alternatives do we need? What kind of work will they need to be able to do to meet the demands, imperatives, and sensibilities of development in the twenty-first century? What lessons can we learn from previous generations of development researchers and practitioners who also sought to forge alternative administrative platforms? We consider some answers to these questions in the final chapter, before concluding in the epilogue with some practical advice for those considering engaging more intentionally with international development issues and organizations.

4

Engaging an Increasingly Complex World: From What We Have to What We Need

The development outcomes achieved over the last seventy years – from roughly 1950 to 2020 – have been extraordinary. The global welfare gains during this period in health, education, poverty reduction, life expectancy, and the reduction of violence exceed those attained in the entirety of previous human history (Pritchett 2022); those gains must be acknowledged by anyone claiming that international development has somehow "failed" or by those who claim to have an alternative approach to development that would be "better." These remarkable achievements, however, were often obtained from a very low base, and, as noted in Chapter 1, the development challenge just keeps getting harder. Going from a world where there were essentially no paved roads, no major bridges, no irrigated fields, no schools, no health clinics, and no immunizations to a world where even a small fraction of the population begin to enjoy these things constitutes, by definition, a major improvement in material well-being.

But the very attainment of these initial outcomes creates a new round of development challenges: even if there are surely many miles of roads left to be paved and water pipes to be laid, the skills, sensibilities, and administrative instruments deployed to do these *technical* tasks are not self-implementing – they cannot teach children, heal the sick, regulate powerful companies, forge equitable partnerships with multinational companies, constrain elite power, ensure "free and fair" elections, mediate disputes, or even just ensure that the roads and pipes are adequately maintained. By way of juxtaposition, these latter *adaptive* tasks[1] can be characterized as deeply complex, in the sense that they are highly discretionary and transaction-intensive, often have to counter powerful incentives dissuading officials from doing their job (bribes, corruption, extortion, routinized indifference), and require the crafting of novel solutions to prevailing problems (because contexts are idiosyncratic and the details of effective solutions are largely unknown, and thus cannot readily be inferred from seemingly similar experiences elsewhere). Sectors such as health, education, agricultural extension, justice, policing, regulation, social work, and land management are replete with such complex aspects. For example, providing farmers with the latest ferti-lizers and seeds is one thing; it is a quite different task to persuade farmers to actually use them (since this will entail forsaking practices much more familiar and thus perceived to be less risky). Building new roads is politically glamorous; maintaining them is decidedly unglamorous – but both aspects are necessary if the development benefits of roads are to be realized and sustained.

To implement this increasingly diverse *range* of tasks, the development challenges of the twenty-first century must incorporate the forging of new, fit-for-purpose administrative systems and leadership styles that can effectively implement responses to both technical and adaptive challenges in ways perceived to be locally legitimate. The call in Sustainable Development Goal #17 to "strengthen the means of imple-mentation" at least creates some rhetorical space for this work. But achieving this strengthening is going to require the crafting of administrative systems able to accommodate the provision of qualitatively different types of support to different types of development problems, and to assess them in correspondingly different kinds of ways (Bain et al. 2016). As noted earlier, our current systems were conceived and enshrined in an age largely focused on filling "object gaps" (physical infrastructure) and then "idea gaps" (schools, policies) (Romer 1993), but, to the extent that these two "gaps" have now been (or in principle at least potentially can be) "filled," the current key challenge is responding effectively to "implementation gaps," especially as they pertain to complex adaptive interventions or complex *aspects* of technical interventions (e.g. slum upgrading, which requires, among other things, both the technical engineering skills needed to construct low-cost housing *and* the extensive adaptive social skills needed to negotiate the terms, costs, and timing of the transition with slum dwellers – who are often poor, undocumented, non-literate in the local language, and deeply skeptical of promises made by political or corporate leaders).[2]

Importantly, this array of increasingly complex implementation tasks is eventually encountered by those engaged in national development, big development, and small development – which is to say, everyone. This chapter explores these dynamics in greater detail, and connects them to current events in international relations, in the process seeking to making a sound, supportable, and implementable case for "doing development differently." Such complementary approaches need not be seen as "radical," nor should they require a major "crisis" to make them salient. The world needs to work with what it has to build the systems it needs: systems that are fit-for-purpose responses to twenty-first-century challenges, deploying twenty-first-century skills, sensibilities, technologies, resources, and local knowledge, in ways that prioritize the concerns of poor countries.

The implementation gap: how reforms succeed at failing[3]

Development is ultimately about enhancing human dignity and opportunity, and committing to active participation in a coherent, compelling, responsive, and legitimate national enterprise. Doing this requires building economic, political, social, and administrative systems capable of undertaking incrementally more complex tasks, reliably and affordably for all. But, as has been stressed at several points in this book (and as current events in Eastern Europe make clear), achieving and sustaining these objectives is a never-ending journey, fraught and precarious, requiring eternal vigilance.

A central operational task for all development strategies, including any would-be paradigmatic "alternative" to prevailing approaches, is facilitating the state's capability to implement increasingly complex and contentious tasks, at scale, for all. Ensuring the state itself is constrained and accountable is perhaps the most difficult task of all. Few now dispute the importance of education, health, water, public finance, security, and justice – these are core responsibilities of the state. But the enduring problem today is that too often students don't learn, doctors don't show up for work, roads and wells are not maintained, supplies arrive intermittently (if at all), and "the law" is either expensive, unenforced, distant, co-opted, or itself the problem. In one sense, development professionals have long fretted over these concerns, but the standard response has been to regard weak implementation capability as a function of either (a) "low capacity" on the part of individual public sector staff, with the concomitant solution being the provision of a raft of "capacity building" training programs and technological "upgrades," or (b) "endemic corruption" and "lack of political will," for which there are few coherent responses other than vague appeals for "good governance" and compliance with international "best practices." Neither consistently effects lasting change (see Box 4.1, and, more generally, Andrews 2013 and Andrews et al. 2017). But in another sense, most development agencies vastly underplay the importance of implementation and context. Over the duration of the typical development intervention, the allocation of talent, effort, resources, and prestige is distinctly bi-modal, with vastly disproportionate amounts of intellectual and political energy expended on ex ante design ("policy") and ex post assessment ("evaluation"), and considerably less given to understanding and responding appropriately to local contextual realities, and refining implementation processes and capabilities in response to emergent challenges.

Box 4.1 Public sector reform in Malawi, 1995–2016

Between 1995 and 2015, the World Bank undertook twenty-nine different projects in Malawi with a thematic focus on public expenditure, financial management, and procurement.[4] Examples of such efforts included large lending projects such as the Fiscal Restructuring and Deregulation Program (which ran in three phases from 1996 until 2002) and the Financial Management, Transparency, and Accountability Project (in operation from 2003 to 2009). They also included non-lending knowledge products such as the Malawi Policy Note series and Public Expenditure review and recipient-executed activities such as the Financial Reporting and Oversight Improvement Program. An analysis of the Public Financial Management (PFM) portfolio limited itself to closed lending projects, of which there were ten that took place between 1995 and 2016. (Conclusions drawn from an assessment of these efforts are therefore specific to lending projects and should not be generalized to all types of instruments.)

Using the ten projects, we began by identifying all the PFM-related indicators within those projects before matching them against their results to see which were achieved and which were not. In this way we sought to gain a picture of what the projects aimed to do and whether they achieved their aims. Broadly speaking, the projects appear to have been fairly successful. From the ten projects, we identified seventy-seven PFM-specific indicators spanning over twenty years;[5] of these seventy-seven, we found that forty-four were classed as having been achieved[6] – yielding a reasonably acceptable success rate of 57 percent.

However, this picture needs to be supplemented by an assessment of whether the aims were actually "functional" – that is, seeking more than merely cosmetic reform focused on "form" (or appearances). To determine functionality, we isolated all the PFM-specific results from our project sample and separated these into results of form only and results which had an impact on underlying function: for our purposes, functional results were defined as those that had a direct impact on one of the four functional objectives proposed by Andrews, Cangiano et al. (2014), namely: (i) prudent fiscal decisions; (ii) credible budgets; (iii) reliable and efficient resource flows and transactions; and (iv) institutional accountability. A result was categorized as "form" if it did not provide evidence of a direct contribution to one of the functional indicators. We found that the majority of what the projects were aiming to achieve was a change in terms of how organizations *appeared*, not in terms of their actual underlying impact on service delivery. Within the seventy-seven PFM-specific indicators we identified, we found a total of fifty-one "form" results and twenty-six "function" results. In short, almost 70 percent of what the projects measured or aimed for was change only in terms of whether institutions *looked like* their functioning counterparts (i.e., had the requisite structures, policies, systems, and laws in place).

World Bank-funded PFM projects also had considerably more success in achieving these "form" results: forty-four of our seventy-seven project indicators were classed as meeting such objectives. Of these forty-four, only ten (23 percent) were classed as functional. While 67 percent of what was aimed at in terms of change in form was met, only 38 percent of our functional aims were met. It appears that demonstrable improvements in actual performance are far harder to achieve than changes that are primarily regulative, procedural, or systems oriented. A mid-term review for a Bank-supported PFM project observes how this discrepancy plays out in practice, noting that "technical solutions (capacity building, procurement of hardware and software) seem to be progressing very well but attempts to improve the control environment are painfully slow – bank reconciliation, commitment control, cash management, unauthorized access to International Financial Management Information Systems (IFMIS)" (World Bank 2015a). Taken as a whole, this distinction means that *only 23 percent of the*

> *projects in this study had a demonstrable impact on under-lying performance*; this is in marked contrast to the initial 57 percent rate of success with which we began. Related measures by the non-profit organization Global Integrity similarly reveal that while Malawi has anticorruption laws, civil service laws, and public management laws (all formal, regulative aspects) whose quality rivals those of developed countries, its scores for implementation are significantly lower than those of developed country counterparts.[7]
>
> Source: Bridges and Woolcock (2017)

There are some encouraging signs that this is changing – for example, "learning" has steadily begun to replace mere "attendance" as the key measure of education attainment (World Bank 2018b)[8] – but it is important to unpack the imperatives shaping how development resources that continue to flow to governments (or other organizations) for the purpose of improving implementation are often assessed as "successful" when in reality they have yielded little actual improvement in performance. In such circumstances, sustaining a flow of resources requires maintaining the *illusion* that implementing agencies are improving, not least to appease those insisting on "evidence" of improvement in the short run as the requirement for continued support. In both cases, a phenomenon known as "isomorphic mimicry" is likely to be on display (Andrews et al. 2017). This has been documented in a range of country contexts. It was first advanced by sociologists of business management in the United States, who noted that "follower" firms often imitated the organizational structures of "lead" firms, in the belief that *looking like* a lead firm would convince potential investors and customers that they were *in fact* (or were on the cusp of becoming) a lead firm.

A similar dynamic is often on display as developing countries seek to reform their public organizations: they pretend to improve (by engaging in various strategies that convey the appearance of change) and donors pretend to believe them (by counting as "success" various indicators that are not actual outcome/performance measures but rather measures of inputs provided or compliance with administrative protocols attained) (Andrews 2013). Exemplifying this point, Pritchett (2014) notes that (at least at the time of his writing) the Indian state of Tamil Nadu had 817 indicators for measuring the delivery of public education, but none that actually assessed whether students were learning; in this instance, an abundance of measurements and data was available on the *inputs* to learning, but these were entirely disconnected from assessing the attainment of (what should have been) the policy's central objective. In short, both governments and development agencies tend to measure form, not function, or erroneously conflate form with function in imagining that the former gives rise to the latter.

Isomorphic mimicry is especially prominent (i.e., likely to exist and difficult to subvert) when efforts to build modern institutions for effective implementation are undertaken in contexts or sectors where social institutions (i.e., social norms, networks, interactions, and organizations) are especially salient. By now it should be readily apparent why this is so: (a) social institutions are often difficult to apprehend or "see" (let alone measure) by outsiders, so insiders who either have a vested interest in stalling reform or (more constructively) are seeking to buy time for reforms to take hold are far better placed to deploy strategies that convince outside development agencies to continue their support; (b) reforming or complementing social institutions is usually a decidedly non-linear, non-uniform, and contentious (hence risky) process, so, under pressure, all parties are likely to defer to "best practice" imperatives (which, by definition, are especially resonant with assessment protocols stressing compliance with such practices over demonstrated accomplishment in situ); and (c) it is the principles of engaging with, rather than the particular design characteristics of, successful social institutional interventions that are likely to be generalizable elsewhere (i.e., to have some external validity).

One of these principles is that, when engaging with highly complex problems, considerable time and effort must be expended on identifying anew, each and every time, the actual problems that implementers confront and the range of plausible, supportable solutions that might work in response to them. Such an approach is hard for dominant organizational structures and incentives to accommodate, however, since they strongly prefer standardized "best practice" or "tool kit" responses, and too often impose too much on too little too soon, thereby not only generating few actual instances of tangible success[9] but also perpetuating a dynamic that, by routinely failing, delegitimizes the very idea of reform while short-circuiting the local learning required to produce context-specific responses to context-specific problems. Moran's (2016) masterful analysis of the Australian government's century-long efforts to engage with Aboriginal populations on social services such as health, education, and housing – efforts that are well funded, often well intentioned, and deploy the latest technologies – documents a lamentable and oft-repeated cycle of what he calls purging, swinging, mimicry, and contradiction: that is, of first declaring the previous policy a failure (no matter what it actually achieved), then layering a vacillating series of instruments and objectives upon one another, often by copying "best practices" from abroad, all of which introduces so many "policies" with so many constituent elements that, almost inevitably, irreconcilable contradictions emerge, thus making life permanently frustrating for providers and recipients alike. Issues such as property rights, which might seem relatively straightforward in most places, are desired and possible in some Aboriginal communities, are an utterly alien concept in others (e.g., those committed to communal ownership of land), and are desirable but unworkable in still others (e.g., those places where overt policies to dismantle communities and then, decades later, reassemble them have completely disrupted a coherent accounting, in both formal records and oral history, of which family lineage has legitimate claim to what land). Our prevailing administrative instruments and imperatives struggle to accommodate such vexing variation.

The challenge of evaluating complex adaptive interventions

Another manifestation of this complex dynamic in action – and another instance of why international development is one of humanity's greatest challenges – becomes apparent when moving from implementation to evaluation; i.e., assessing whether and how adaptive interventions, wholly or in part, achieve their goals.[10] The challenge for those wishing to argue for (or against) the effectiveness of more adaptive approaches is that their success or failure cannot always be measured with tools designed to measure more traditional approaches. Since the imperative to be accountable cannot (and should not) be avoided, how then can one discern and demonstrate whether or not adaptive efforts are working?

Lessons from a study of a major health intervention in various states across Nigeria provide insights into both the problem and a possible solution (see Bridges and Woolcock 2019). In this intervention – the Saving One Million Lives Project (SOML) – an adaptive approach was applied to one particular aspect of it, in which a technical assistance (TA) firm hired and trained front-line implementers to identify and solve local problems pertaining to the delivery and uptake of key inputs to the government's six priority health targets. In turn, the eight states in which this approach was deployed, along with the TA firm itself, were incrementally funded to the extent these six specific health outcomes (immunization, nutrition, HIV/AIDS, family planning, maternal health, malaria) moved in a positive direction *at the state level*. Somehow, the primary players in this drama found themselves tasked with trying to discern the effectiveness of one aspect (local-level problem-solving) of one project (SOML) by its impact on aggregate state-level health outcomes.

That such an expectation could be established and regarded as reasonable itself says a lot about the inherent challenges of international development, in which there is an enduring mismatch between the vast and expanding array of complex problems to be addressed on the one hand, and, on the other, a seemingly small and shrinking array of theories and methods by which responses to them can be rigorously but usefully assessed. Moreover, this space shrinks still further when the very term "rigorous" itself gets monopolized by those privileging one evaluation approach (most conspicuously, randomized controlled trials) over all others. Such an approach can be exactly right for very particular kinds of interventions yet be of limited salience for the vast majority of important development problems (Deaton and Cartwright 2018), especially those that are "complex" in the way I have defined them here.

Adaptive approaches can and should be assessed against the key claims they make, which are usually twofold: (1) that such approaches can fix problems that matter, and (2) that in doing so they build problem-solving skills. With regard to the critical question "Did we fix the problem?," one of the issues in the Nigeria case was the difficulty of deciding what level of "problem fixed" (e.g., national or local; whole of government or departmental) equated to success of the approach. In practice, success was primarily judged on the attainment of the six state-wide aggregate health outcomes, and the firm selected to facilitate the adaptive approach was given a performance-based contract, with a third of their payment made conditional on achievement of these state-wide increases across these six outcomes (as measured by yearly surveys) in the eight states where they were operating.

The intent to have a clear measure of problem fixed is welcome, but were *state-level* health outcomes the right measure? The assemblage required to shift state-level health outcomes in Nigeria (and everywhere else) comprises a vast array of intertwined political, economic, and social factors. Some of these factors are observable (pre-existing policies, donor programs, funding levels, political priorities), while others are statistically unobservable (political favors, leadership quality, cultural issues, personality clashes). Collectively, these factors shape outcomes from both the supply and demand sides. On the supply side, we find factors relating to where money goes, how reliably and frequently staff are paid, how diligently they work, and so forth. On the demand side are factors that include whether people use birth control, immunize and adequately feed their children, sleep under mosquito nets, or consult maternal health professionals, among many other behaviors. Together, this vast assemblage of factors comprises what Bridges and I came to refer to, during our research, as the "elephant." All else considered, the elephant is likely to be by far the greatest determinant of aggregate outcomes – just as national development, as described in previous chapters, is the primary driver of a country's (and thus its citizens') welfare.

By contrast, we compared the country-wide, World Bank-supported health intervention under which these six outcomes were being targeted to a bird on the back of the elephant. (A commissioner we interviewed in one of the states likened their efforts under the intervention to "pouring a cup of tea into an ocean" – a reference to the ways that political machinations around civil servant pay were, at that time, overwhelming any possible program impact.) To complete our fauna analogy, the adaptive component, funded at just 0.1 percent of the total intervention budget, was compared to a fly on the back of the bird. In the states that received this assistance, the overall movement in the six key aggregate indicators can thus be said to have been driven by the combined influence of a fly, a bird, and an elephant. (And massive contextual differences across the states mean that we really had different flies on different birds on different elephants!) Thus, whatever movement we see in these indicators, positive or otherwise, cannot and should not be attributed to the fly alone.

The analogy isn't perfect, but the point is this: yes, adaptive approaches should be judged on their ability to fix problems, but those judgments of success must be closely aligned with the actual problems that the approach itself directly addresses. While the measures of success in the Nigeria case were at the state level, the problems the adaptive approach was actually working on were necessarily far more discrete and localized, due to the targeted nature and relatively small scale of the assistance. These problems included issues like "people in X area use the bed nets we distribute for fishing so that they can catch fish to eat and sell"; "health workers haven't been paid for the past six months so they charge for services that should be free"; "religious leaders in this locality are opposed to the use of contraceptives, so women either don't use them or don't report such use"; "health workers are absent because doctors have been kidnapped in the past"; and a host of others. It was on these kinds of localized, discrete manifestations of the problem that the "fly" – the adaptive assistance – focused its efforts. We argue that in judging the success of the fly's efforts, evaluation should likewise focus on movements at this level.[11]

Of course, one may still reasonably assume that the fixing of these discrete, local-level issues will progressively combine to shift state-wide health outcome indicators, but as with any theory of change, the assumption that "flies" can help move "elephants" requires testing. And demonstrating causation here will be tough. While it is reasonable to expect to be able to discern effects that are closely coupled with the change (e.g., to see whether a designated solution to the issue of religious leaders' opposition to contraception did in fact result in greater use of contraceptives in that locality), it does not follow that that same solution – even if unambiguously and wildly successful in resolving the localized problem – can be causally connected to changes (or not) in the aggregate outcomes of contraceptive use at a state-wide level. There are just too many links in the chain – or, to put it differently, the vast amount of "noise" in large complex systems drowns out whatever "signal" may be emanating from a particular location. Even if the vast assemblage of factors ultimately does come together to shift a state-wide indicator, the trajectory of change in such complex interventions is rarely linear (Woolcock 2019c, 2022), the specific contribution of the adaptive component will be almost impossible to isolate empirically, and it will most likely (by definition, by virtue of being responsive to contextual idiosyncrasies) be non-uniform (meaning that it will violate one of the key requirements of an experiment).[12]

The specific case of assessing community-driven development interventions

A similar challenge, and corresponding contention, surrounds efforts to ascertain the effectiveness of Community-Drive Development (CDD) projects, the largest-scale attempts to incorporate local communities into decisions pertaining to their welfare, harnessing their knowledge and collective judgment to prioritize problems, assess the merits of proposed solutions, and ultimately to select how finite development resources should be allocated.[13] Pioneered in Indonesia in 1997 in the aftermath of the fall of the New Order government (see Box 4.2), over 190 CDD programs have since been implemented in seventy-eight countries ranging from Sierra Leone to Afghanistan to Cambodia (Wong and Guggenheim 2018). But do they "work"? That seemingly reasonable question – one rightly asked of road-building projects, tax cuts, cash transfers, and child sponsorship programs – is not the most fruitful for assessing highly complex interventions like CDD because the answer is always and everywhere, "It depends." Why? Because virtually every design characteristic of a CDD project will be the opposite of, say, a project to introduce nutrition supplements: CDD projects are deeply complex and non-uniform (beyond shared general principles); their constituent mechanisms are numerous, loose, and hard to specify/measure; they are highly sensitive (by design) to idiosyncratic contextual realities; and they require highly competent, persistent, and discerning implementers who are especially deft at mediating potentially contentious disputes. As such, CDD projects are inherently fated to always and everywhere generate results that are "mixed." Put differently, twenty years from now another meta-review of CDD projects will be conducted, and it too will doubtless conclude that the "evidence is mixed."

Fortunately, adding but a single word to the standard evaluation question yields insights that can teach everyone – but especially senior managers, designers, evaluators, researchers, and donors – how to think more accurately,

Box 4.2 The Kecamatan Development Program, Indonesia

A defining feature of CDD programs is their use of open community forums – not external technical experts, government officials, religious authorities, respected elders, local leaders, committees, or lotteries – to allocate finite development resources. In these forums, small groups present their proposals for a certain "public good" project (which must meet certain criteria; e.g., it cannot be used for religious purposes), with fellow community members publicly assessing its merits on the basis of criteria such as its prospects for being completed on time and on budget, for being able to be maintained after completion, and for addressing a high-priority local development problem. Such forums are, among other things, a pragmatic response to the reality that the demand for development funds will likely always exceed supply, and thus that a mechanism of some kind must be found to prioritize certain projects over others.

To do this difficult work, the mechanism must enjoy shared legitimacy among all participants, especially those groups whose time-consuming efforts to prepare a proposal are ultimately rejected in favor of others. These design characteristics were a distinctive feature of the world's first national-level CDD program – Indonesia's Kecamatan Development Project (KDP), which began in the late 1990s and continues to this day (though it has changed names several times, expanded its reach, and undergone numerous procedural refinements along the way, in 2014 becoming nationally enshrined as the "Village Law"[14]). Importantly, the choice of community forums as the mechanism for allocating finite resources emerged from an extensive prior research effort – the Local Level Institutions (LLI) Study – to better understand how Indonesia's local-level institutions functioned. Multiple waves of the LLI study have since been conducted (see Wetterberg et al. 2013).

In the aftermath of the fall of the New Order government in 1997, two existential development challenges had to be addressed simultaneously: (1) in the short run, how to get financial resources to the most vulnerable communities across the country in the midst of a debilitating economic crisis; and (2) in the medium run, how to establish a new "social contract" between citizens and the state in a fledgling democracy. Having previously declared Indonesia the "jewel in its crown" (Guggenheim 2006), the World Bank's credibility as a leader on these twin issues in the aftermath of the country's collapse (precipitated by the Asian financial crisis) was considerably compromised. Fortuitously, however, the LLI study provided the knowledge base on which to address both challenges in ways that were new, innovative, and yet also distinctively Indonesian (i.e., not based on putative "best practices" borrowed or copied from elsewhere). Given the high stakes at the time – primarily for Indonesia but also for the World Bank – ensuring the legitimacy and credibility of the proposed approach was vital.

Drawing on the findings from the LLI study, the central design premise was to forge a policy response built on prevailing social institutions. In the KDP, this entailed adapting a strong Indonesian civic custom known as *gotong royong*, which affirms that a good Indonesian citizen is one who actively contributes to their community's well-being. By explicitly incorporating this familiar social practice, the operational "wager" was that villagers would impute legitimacy to a process that, though contentious by design, would be able to introduce – for the first time in most adult Indonesians' lives – a procedure for allocating finite development resources in an open, transparent, rules-driven, and merit-based way. A subsequent large-scale research project undertaken to assess the effectiveness of this "wager" found numerous instances of conflict generated by development projects, and identified various pathways by which conflict could be generated, but found no instances in which conflict associated with the KDP itself had become violent – in stark contrast to other programmatic and policy interventions (Barron et al. 2011; further findings from this study are provided below).

fruitfully, and constructively about what is distinctive and unique about CDD interventions vis-à-vis mainstream development projects, thus what must be correspondingly distinctive and unique about how they are assessed, and thus how claims about specific instances of them are made and (especially) generalized. Rather than asking, "Does X work?" – where X can be not only CDD but "participation," or "empowerment," or "inclusion," or "justice reform," or "Truth and Reconciliation" – just adding the word "When" to the start of the question puts the entire framing into a space able to generate vastly more useful and interesting answers (Woolcock 2019a). Asking *"When* does CDD work?" gives rise to answers that are both more empirically accurate and surely more actionable for managers, donors, policymakers, practitioners, participants, and researchers.

Numerous reviews have shown that CDD *can* work (not that it *does* work – it's an important difference), even in fragile and violent contexts such as Afghanistan (see Casey 2018). But showing that it *can* work just begs the question, "Under what conditions does CDD work?" Barron et al. (2011), for example, show that the Kecamatan Development Project was able to generate positive impacts (a) when facilitators were selected, trained, managed, and socialized to do the endlessly difficult work of mediating the questions, concerns, and frustrations that resulted from the KDP process (which was novel for villagers, and itself based on contestation, since it required a finite pot of money to be allocated on the basis of merit and transparency, thus explicitly creating "winners" and "losers"); (b) when local elites bought into the new deliberative agenda, not regarding it as a threat to their status even though it required many of them to relinquish personal privileges they had enjoyed under the New Order regime; (c) when the broader social, economic, and political context was conducive to the means (public deliberation) and ends (public goods provision of various kinds) that were being funded by the KDP; and (d) when participants acquired positive problem-solving practices and precedents that spilled over into more everyday (non-project) development challenges, thereby greatly reducing the incidence of violent conflict in the KDP vis-à-vis matched non-KDP villages.[15] Meeting these conditions, or even just some of them, is really hard, which explains why there is such heterogeneity in outcomes; it remains an open empirical question as to whether these, or other, conditions are what explain variation in outcomes in CDD projects elsewhere.

These particular evaluation concerns come to a head when an evaluation of a prominent CDD project, or a certain aspect of it, concludes that it "doesn't work," which then risks sliding into a broader inference that "we have shown that CDD projects don't work." If such sentiments start being internalized by senior managers, entire portfolios of activity, not to mention hundreds of careers, are suddenly vulnerable. However, desperately trying to show that CDD-type projects "work" in the same way that immunizations or infrastructure "work" is doomed to disappointment; the battle cannot and should not be fought on those terms. A key reason is that the underlying impact trajectory for CDD-type interventions is likely to be highly non-linear – and potentially non-uniformly non-linear, making it decidedly difficult to discern what outcomes can reasonably be expected by when. For example, Casey et al. concluded, on the basis of an otherwise stellar ("rigorous") methodology, that a CDD project in Sierra Leone (GoBifo) created "positive short-run effects on local public goods and economic outcomes," but found "no evidence for sustained impacts on collective action, decision-making, or the involvement of marginalized groups, suggesting that the intervention did not durably reshape local institutions" (2012: 1755) – which quickly leads most readers to the seductive but wildly inaccurate conclusion: "We now know that CDD programs are good at providing services and infrastructure but that they don't improve social cohesion."

"We" only "know" this if we have decidedly unwarranted assumptions underpinning our understanding of when and how different *types* of development intervention unfold – e.g., that "improvements" in roads and communities can reasonably be expected to occur at the same rate over the

same trajectory (they can't, because they don't) – and zero
sense of the conditions under which CDD results obtained
in one context might travel to another or be successfully
scaled up. If changes in social organizations take place over
many years, perhaps decades, then a typical evaluation cycle
– spanning, say, three to five years between baseline and
follow-up data – will simply not be sufficient time for any
of these changes to have transpired, let alone be measured.
Moreover, it may well be that any given CDD project is in
fact totally failing at "building social cohesion," but if it
really does take a generation to see any kind of observable
social change in this space in this context, even a perfect
randomized controlled experiment conducted over just four
years is not going to be able to tell the difference, if a null
result is found, between a CDD project that is an "actual
failure" (and thus should be halted immediately) and one
for which observers, implementers, and participants alike
should instead "just be patient and persistent." As we noted
in the previous chapter, in the absence of an underlying
theory of change informing reasoned expectations about
the trajectory and timeframes of impact *in any particular
instance*, competing claims about both general and specific
efficacy are largely unresolvable. They become especially
salient and consequential, however, when claims are made
about the effects of "social anything" (CDD, participation,
accountability) on "social something" (social capital, social
cohesion, social inclusion, the social contract, etc.).

In such interventions, the quality of design and implementation, along with layers of contextual idiosyncrasy explicitly
seeking to be accommodated, all combine to generate highly
variable outcomes. Which one of these factors, singularly
or in combination, is most salient is an empirical question,
but not one that standard "rigorous" impact evaluations are
designed to answer. Rather than trying to discern the average
"effects of causes," an alternative approach is to seek instead
to identify "causes of effects," a distinction first made by
John Stuart Mill in the nineteenth century. One pragmatic
way to do this is to exploit the likelihood of variation in the
quality of (say) economic growth and public service delivery,

especially when an operational space is characterized by identical policies, salaries, and career incentives (as, e.g., in most Middle East countries[16]). This spatial variation in outcomes, in turn, can serve as a basis for identifying, explaining, and sharing instances of implementation success, and can be deployed at units of analysis ranging from subnational regions and government ministries to individual clinics and schools (see McDonnell 2020). Since this observed outcome variation cannot be a function of "policy" (since one has effectively held it constant), it is much more likely to be a product of connectedness, complementarities, implementation capability, and contextual characteristics, all of which accord a prominent place to the influence of social institutions. Engaging with and understanding these realities will require a coherently integrated package of theory and research methods (Woolcock 2019c; Copestake et al. 2019; Rao 2022; Rogers and Woolcock 2023). This is especially the case for those policies and programs that inherently require a multitude of interacting social institutional arrangements (e.g., repeated face-to-face interactions) for their very delivery, such as classroom teaching, social work, local justice, and curative health care. Even in the field of economic growth, recent research on subnational variation in Mexico reveals how widely variable local growth rates can be, and how important social networks are in connecting communities to diversified factor and product markets (Hausmann et al. 2021).

In this type of analytical approach, the basis of reform and policy advice is not the adoption of generic "best practice" lessons imported from abroad, but the outcomes that the most innovative and effective local actors have already obtained. The basic premise is that someone, somewhere, somehow has already figured out how to optimize within the current policy and political constraints; a key role for external actors is to help identify who and where these people are, to celebrate them, to draw on their legitimacy and credibility as change agents, and to give them a platform to explain to their colleagues (or fellow citizens) how they might do likewise. Importantly, discerning how to optimize within prevailing constraints is the first step in a strategy that ultimately seeks to "unbind" these constraints and extend the implementation capability frontier; in difficult environments in particular, such as "fragile states," it also helps to demonstrate that modest – sometimes extraordinary – success can be obtained in unlikely situations (see, among others, Barma et al. 2014 and April et al. 2018).[17]

The longstanding quest for an alternative aid architecture[18]

Whether it is a matter of building large administrative systems from scratch or reforming existing ones, astute observers of national development dynamics have long recognized that certain key aspects of such processes are legal/technical in nature, and thus readily amenable to discrete specialized inputs from professionalized experts (e.g., lawyers, accountants, economists, engineers). More broadly, a central task of professional associations is to discern, certify, and (as necessary) enforce "best practices" – i.e., standardized (often codified) procedures that, when faithfully deployed, reliably yield the desired outcome (Behn 2017). Adopting "best practices," by definition, spares reformers the need to waste time and money experimenting with alternatives: adoptees need only to be trained in the new procedures for efficiency gains to be duly realized. But these same observers have also been quick to stress that while adopting certain "best practice" elements may be very necessary, they are also very insufficient: successful organizational reform, at scale, requires engaging with large numbers of people and their associated (and often highly idiosyncratic) identities, values, motivations, incentives, aspirations, fears, preferences, abilities, and obligations. Moreover, where there are people there is politics: hierarchies, power, resources, and rules whose salience is only partially capturable – or in Scott's (1998) delightful phrase, "rendered legible" – by formal administrative instruments such as contracts, forms, budgets, organizational charts, and reporting lines (important and necessary as these may be). Apprehending and discerning the significance of the "illegible" aspects of organizational performance requires deploying different research methods that in turn inform different support strategies for navigating the reform process.

This summation broadly captures the key insights formalized in classic works at the nexus of public administration, planning, and development that have appeared roughly each decade from the 1950s onwards. The scholarly work began with Charles Lindblom (1959, 1979), who famously argued that "muddling through," inelegant as it may sound, was likely to be the optimal strategy for navigating complex reform processes. Thereafter Hirschman (1968)[19] spelled out these challenges in more granular detail, using "live" development projects as spaces wherein observers could (a) assess the peculiar dynamics shaping how general administrative principles were actually put into practice in particular places, and (b) infer, on the basis of these experiences, broader principles for development theory, policy, and strategy. Hirschman's insightful observations explaining, for example, why projects *always* cost more money and take more time than anticipated was borne of a corresponding long-term perspective wherein the array of net benefits of these same projects was also unanticipated in the planning stages, as was the fact that implementers proved consistently adept at solving problems along the way. Tweaking Adam Smith, Hirschman called this conjuncture of mechanisms the "principle of the hiding hand."

Subsequent work by Flyvbjerg and Sunstein (2015) assessing a sample of over 300 major projects sought to show empirically that such "beneficence" on the part of planners appears in fact to be a relatively rare phenomena; vastly more common – 2.5 times more likely, they find – was a "malevolent" form of the "hiding hand," in which large projects consistently missed performance targets because of predation on budgets and contracts by unscrupulous participants. With a vastly larger data base, however, Williams (2017) drew on a sample of 14,000 development projects in Ghana and found that a third of them "failed" – a result, he argues, less of corruption or clientelism than of perennial collective action challenges, manifest in particular in public financial management issues. Whatever the ratio of beneficence to malevolence in the planning/management of development projects generally (or specifically), for present purposes the two enduring points are that effective implementation matters, and that it includes forging a robust organizational capability to resolve (to professional standards) unanticipated – and indeed unanticipate-able[20] – problems. The important recent work by Honig (2018), conducted on an even larger database of projects from around the world, reaches a similar conclusion, noting in particular that the more complex an intervention and the more space it is given to make mid-course corrections, the more successful it is likely to be.

Concerns with the limits of modern planning systems continued in the 1970s, and were voiced in a seminal paper by Rittel and Webber (1973). Here again we find a deep frustration with the abiding mismatch between what prevailing administrative systems are designed to do (i.e., manage narrow, codifiable tasks) and the broad array of (idiosyncratic, non-codifiable) tasks they are routinely asked to do. "[W]e are all beginning to realize," Rittel and Webber lamented

> that one of the most intractable problems is that of defining problems (of knowing what distinguishes an observed condition from a desired condition) and of locating problems (finding where in the complex causal network the trouble really lies). In turn, and equally intractable, is the problem of identifying the actions that might effectively narrow the gap between what-is and what-ought-to-be. (1973: 159)

Squeezing such challenges into a single administrative apparatus is doomed to disappointment, they argued, because "the problems of governmental planning – and especially those of social or policy planning – are ill-defined; and they rely upon elusive political judgment for resolution. (Not 'solution.' Social problems are never solved. At best they are only re-solved – over and over again" [1973: 160]).

In the 1980s, such enduring discontent prompted Rondinelli to argue that "international assistance programmes for developing countries are in urgent need of revision," precisely because of the inherent "uncertainty and complexity of the development process," the levels and forms of which could not be adequately accommodated by the dominant planning systems. Instead, he maintained, development projects should be regarded as "policy experiments" – that is, as specific instantiations of ideas "that facilitate innovation, responsiveness and experimentation," thereby promoting "decision-making processes that join learning with action" (1983: xx, xx, viii). Later that decade, Brinkerhoff and Ingle (1989) sought to articulate a hybrid "structured flexibility approach" to development administration, one that integrated what they called the "blueprint" model (characterized by "highly detailed pre-implementation plans rigidly applied") and the "process" model (emphasizing "building problem-solving capacity" while taking an "iterative learning orientation"), arguing that this was the approach most likely to facilitate the "adaptive management" capabilities needed "to deal with uncertain and changing task environments" (1989: 487).

In the 1990s, Uphoff (1992) provided a detailed concrete example of such an experiment in development design and implementation, showing how a dedicated team had eschewed "Newtonian" social science[21] in a project to rebuild one of Sri Lanka's largest and most conflict-ridden irrigation systems. In an influential textbook on governance and administration in development, Turner and Hulme (1997) explicitly created space for "adaptive administration." More broadly, Scott (1998) showed that the widespread deployment of "high-modernist" logic in the post-colonial period – manifest most conspicuously in deference to foreign expertise (especially in agriculture, finance, and land management)[22] and the introduction of new managerial systems of public administration, all in the name of promoting national development – could only ever partially "render legible" the deep cultural and institutional diversity on which such sectoral activities rest.

As such, these reforms, and the development projects to which they gave rise, mostly only helped fledgling governments to "see like a state" rather than build local legitimacy and actual functionality. In being able to "see" but not "act," however, they ended up "looking like a state" (Pritchett et al. 2013) while too often failing to function like one.

Anchored, as it were, by Hirschman, we can thus see an oft-repeated claim spanning the planning and public administration literature in the second half of the twentieth century (and beyond), namely that purposively modernizing economies, societies, and polities via development policies and projects is a highly complex undertaking – so complex, in fact, that a single administrative system (and underlying logic) can only get you so far. As useful as they may be for certain technical tasks, there are real limits to the extent to which logframes and the like can be expected to engage with adaptive challenges, the presence of which becomes both more ubiquitous and more consequential as development itself takes place. Such challenges require a different approach, hints of which can be seen in specific cases (such as Uphoff's Gal Oya irrigation project, and much of the work on common-pool resource management that netted Elinor Ostrom a Nobel Prize), especially where success has occurred in unlikely places.

My own work with Matt Andrews, Salimah Samji, and Lant Pritchett has endeavored to both articulate and instantiate an alternative operational approach to public sector reform, which we have called Problem-Driven Iterative Adaptation (PDIA). Building on the antecedent ideas laid out above, but grounded in a more urgent empirical concern about the mostly stagnant or declining levels of public sector implementation capability in today's developing countries – concerns made all the more pressing by the increasing complexity of contemporary public sector challenges, by heightened citizen expectations of their national governments (embodied in the language of the SDGs), and by the likelihood of populations doubling in Africa by 2050 – we attempt to provide a practical response strategy for complex implementation challenges.[23] This strategy, ideally taken on by teams within a public sector department, is based on four applied principles, each of which stands in rather stark contrast to the prevailing approaches used by most national governments and big development agencies: (1) local solutions for local problems; (2) pushing problem-driven positive deviance; (3) try, learn, iterate, adapt; (4) scale through diffusion. Since its inception a decade ago, PDIA has been deployed in sectors and contexts ranging from police reform in Afghanistan and public sector leadership in Cambodia to maternal health in India and small-business creation for women in Mozambique. It's most widespread use has been in public financial management reform in several African countries, where a recent independent assessment has concluded that while "PDIA is not a silver bullet" it has nonetheless "proven itself to be a valuable instrument in the PFM reform toolkit."[24]

But, alas, all this work over all these decades remains marginal to contemporary mainstream development theory, policy, practice, and research. Why? Why has such a clear, longstanding, oft-repeated, and compelling account of a central development challenge, complemented by (the broad outlines of) a coherent and supportable alternative, largely failed to dislodge the orthodoxy? Three broad answers logically suggest themselves. First, the work of Hirschman and his followers, while perhaps compelling on the surface, may nonetheless contain fatal flaws that, in time, have rendered it intellectually and/or operationally suspect. If so, perhaps fledgling alternatives have just inexorably collapsed under their own weight, inherently unable to deliver on their promises. A second possibility is that Hirschman et al.'s work has inadequately engaged dominant approaches and disciplinary practices (especially those of economics) on terms demanding a more serious hearing. From this perspective, Hirschmanian development has remained marginal, whether by design or default, not because it is fundamentally unsound but because it has failed to convey its central analytical and empirical claims using the methods and models demanded of everyone else. A third answer could be that, despite robust evidence and adequate communication, thinkers from

Lindblom onwards have spoken primarily to – and sought their legitimacy from – a niche academic audience, winning admiring followers on campus on the "supply side" of ideas production across successive generations, but never seeking to build a sizeable and politically influential "demand side" constituency in the corridors of power where key decisions affecting development policy and practice are made. Put differently, perhaps Hirschman et al. have been too concerned with "preaching to the choir" rather than having the courage of their convictions and seeking to forge a large base of active support among those actually "doing" development.

Which of these three responses provides the best answer? The first option, while plausible, has little basis in the literature – researchers may quibble with or outright challenge some of Hirschman's key ideas, but no one denies his originality and deeply insightful way of engaging with development issues. Indeed, Hirschman's work remains one of the best in social science to "think with": of the thousands of books or articles ever published with the words "economic development" in the title, Hirschman's (1958) *The Strategy of Economic Development* is ranked fourth, with over 16,000 citations since its publication.[25] And if operationalizing his approach continues to be an enduring challenge, I suggest this says more about the entrenched nature of incumbent approaches than it does about the intellectual veracity of potential rivals. The very durability of Hirschmanian development theory (albeit at a relatively modest scale) implies that it is highly unlikely it will ever be empirically refuted (at least as this winnowing process usually transpires in "normal science").

The second option, however, has more traction. Perhaps the most stinging critique of Hirschman and his followers was offered by Paul Krugman (1994) in a (in)famous article called "The Fall and Rise of Development Economics." For Krugman, the fatal flaw in Hirschman's approach was not his ideas per se – which Krugman both admired in principle and argued had, over time, been largely vindicated; rather, it was Hirschman's unwillingness and (seeming) inability to formalize his key ideas into clean mathematic models, the hallmark and lingua franca of serious economic theory. In one particularly graphic passage, Krugman asserted that Hirschman (and other producers of what Krugman called "high development theory," such as Gunnar Myrdal) had "rejected ... a willingness to do violence to the richness and complexity of the real world in order to produce controlled, silly models that illustrate key concepts." Such a stance, Krugman argued, had led Hirschman into a self-imposed "intellectual exile," a product of having "proudly gathered up his followers and led them into the wilderness ... Unfortunately, they perished there" (1994: 40).

What to make of this critique, nearly thirty years on? If economics dominates development research (as it does),[26] and if the use of formal models defines "serious" economic work (as it does), then the reluctance/refusal of Hirschmanian social science to play by these rules is a mark of either weakness or constrained strength. It is weakness if such work can and should be modelled in relatively conventional terms, but in eschewing this approach cedes the vastly greater influence it might otherwise have; it is constrained strength if collapsing such work into the strictures of formal models really would "do violence to the richness and complexity of the real world," thereby diluting its substantive force and distinctiveness. Reasonable observers can support either view (or perhaps elements of both), but together they have left Hirschmanian social science playing only a marginal role in shaping mainstream development theory, research, policy, and practice.

My own view aligns mostly with the third option, namely that the enduring marginality of work inspired by Hirschman is a function of failing to prioritize building out a complementary social movement among development practitioners (especially in national governments), drawing on *their* collective experience and expertise to demonstrate its operational utility. Intellectual coherence and empirical support are very necessary but very insufficient bases on which to bring about political and administrative change; it also requires active and growing support from those who will do most of the day-to-day work of authorizing (financially, politically, legally, administratively) and implementing whatever the alternative(s) turn out to be. The scholarly merit of Hirschman-inspired work has stood the test of time – indeed, as noted above, one could say its importance only continues to rise – and has done so by retaining its structure and communicative style (rather than forcing itself into the vernacular of mainstream economics).

The task ahead is to take advantage of the vastly lower costs of global outreach (made possible by the internet and social media) to harness the energy and insights of those best placed to build a twenty-first-century administrative infrastructure using twenty-first-century tools and technologies for responding to twenty-first-century development challenges – namely, practitioners. After six decades, the critiques of orthodoxy are well established, as are the core principles that should guide what comes after it: the missing link in the change process is harnessing the wellspring of largely untapped energy, ideas, skills, and experiences from the implementers and recipients of development projects, so that they can own and construct whatever comes next. Paradoxically, perhaps, it might be said that followers of Hirschman's approach inadequately appreciated that gaining more operational traction for that approach was itself a type of problem requiring their ideas to embark upon, and be refined by, "a long voyage of discovery."

Conclusion

Beyond the need for alternative aid architectures, the broader looming question in the coming decades is the extent to which the world will continue to offer sustained material and political support for national development and instantiate ways to make globalization work for all. Chiseled in stone, literally, in front of the United Nations building in New York City is a passage from the Biblical book of Isaiah, written some 2,700 years ago: "They shall beat their swords into plowshares, and their spears into pruning hooks: nation shall not lift up sword against nation, neither shall they learn war any more." Such an inscription seeks to present the UN, and multilateralism more generally, as the institutional embodiment and fulfillment of humanity's ancient dream of widespread peace and prosperity. And judged by the standards of the world before 1945, a strong case can be made that, for all its inherent problems and limitations, modern multilateralism has been a resounding success. As Kagan aptly summarizes it:

> Until 1945 the story of humankind going back thousands of years was a long tale of war, tyranny, and poverty. Moments of peace were fleeting, democracy so rare as to seem almost accidental, and prosperity the luxury of the powerful few. Our own era has not lacked its horrors, its genocides, its oppressions, its barbarisms. Yet by historical standards, including the standards of the recent past, it has been a relative paradise. Between 1500 and 1945 scarcely a year passed when the strongest powers in the world, the great powers of Europe, were not at war, but since 1945 there have been no wars between the great powers ... Since the end of the Second World War the world has also enjoyed a period of prosperity unlike any other, with more than seven decades of global GDP growth averaging almost 3.5 percent a year ... Since 1945, some four billion people around the world have climbed out of poverty. The number of democratic governments has grown from no more than a dozen in 1939 to more than a hundred today. (2018: 3–4)

One can readily concede that multilateralism is not solely responsible for these achievements and yet still recognize that its contribution was (and remains) seminal. There was nothing "inevitable" or readily predictable about these extraordinary accomplishments; history's arc doesn't bend inexorably towards "progress," and in the aftermath of World War II human beings didn't suddenly "become less violent, less warlike, more caring, more open" (Kagan 2018: 8). These unprecedented outcomes were instead the product of a firm commitment to a calculated wager, namely that

international law, mediated through international organizations comprising the near-universal membership of the
world's sovereign nations, backed by strong military (and
financial) support from the United States and strategic efforts
to incorporate Germany and Japan into global markets
(rather than impose punitive reparations), would ultimately
make for a more open, safer, and broadly prosperous world.

Seventy-five years on, however, there are few people now
alive who can actively remember life before the liberal world
order, and seemingly fewer still who can imagine what the
absence of such an order – its inherent limits and short-
comings notwithstanding – would in all likelihood mean for
life today and the foreseeable future. The many benefits that
stem from multilateralism, in short, are now mostly taken for
granted, leaving them vulnerable to attack from those who
glibly and grossly inflate its costs (and/or its ineffectiveness)
and devalue its many (often unseen and unappreciated)
benefits. Across the western world, and elsewhere, multilateralism's very existence is now being not merely questioned,
but actively challenged.

Following the recent seventy-fifth anniversary of modern
multilateralism, it is thus a timely opportunity to reflect on
the many and varied ways in which multilateralism itself
has changed (or not) over this period. Indeed, the founding
organizations of today's multilateral system – the United
Nations, the European Union, the General Agreement on
Tariffs and Trade, the Food and Agriculture Organization,
the World Bank, and the International Monetary Fund – are
themselves products of two previous attempts, the Concert of
Europe (1815–54, an agreement between the major European
powers to prevent a recurrence of the Napoleonic Wars)[27]
and the League of Nations (1920–46, forged in the aftermath
of World War I). It is crucial to recognize that these efforts,
noble in intent as they may have been, ultimately failed
when it mattered: World War I unfolded when legacy agreements of the Concert of Europe could not hold, while the
package of responses to World War I, of which the League
of Nations was the centerpiece, are now largely regarded as
having sown the seeds for the Great Depression, the rise of

fascism in Germany, and the outbreak of World War II. In 1944, at the height of that war, there was thus precious little evidence – empirically, and in the lived experience of the key participants – that multilateralism "worked"; if anything, it transparently did not. Only committed leadership on the part of Roosevelt and Churchill (in negotiations with Stalin) made it possible for the allied powers to, in effect, double down on the idea that the prevention of future global conflagrations required global organizations with the necessary global membership, legitimacy, resources, instruments, and power.[28] As I write, the war in Ukraine presents perhaps the biggest challenge to multilateralism in its history.

Today's multilateral system has several other pillars: the North Atlantic Treaty Organization, the Association of Southeast Asian Nations, the African Union, the regional development banks, and other efforts to build regional multilateral organizations to promote development, manage trade relations, and build strategic alliances. The most visible of these is probably the European Union: the ruined arena of great wars from past centuries is today, less than sixty years after the establishment of the first limited free trading block in Europe, perceived to be a haven of peace, prosperity, and stability. The extent to which EU countries have delegated the traditional core powers of sovereigns to the community is a marked achievement in today's world and represents a high level of multilateralism.

Thus, at seventy-five, it is worthwhile not only to consider how multilateralism has changed – and, in turn, how it has shaped global development – but also to draw on these experiences to discern in what ways substantive changes might be needed to keep multilateralism vibrant, supported, and effective in the twenty-first century, especially as an agent of national development. Such outcomes cannot be presumed – after all, in 1890, at seventy-five, a dispassionate observer would most likely have concluded that the Concert of Europe was holding up reasonably well. The coming decades could continue to be spectacularly good for human welfare or tragically disappointing; social, economic, and political institutions will continue to be at the epicenter, and grappling with them will shape, as it always has shaped, whichever outcome (or complex mixture of outcomes) prevails.

In this sense – to extend and conclude with the opening epigraph from Paul Virilio – national development presents us with both the ship and shipwreck; that is, with the opportunity to explore, share, and mutually enrich, but also with the accompanying risks of losing our way, squandering our accomplishments, being overwhelmed by storms, hording our gains, crashing, and sinking. Which outcome will prevail is our collective choice to make, to forge, sustain, maintain, and enhance. On a good day, development offers the world an opportunity to decide what constitutes a "better" ship, to finance, build, and maintain it, to minimize the risk of devastating shipwrecks, and to enhance the material well-being of all who elect to travel on it. But doing any of that will be hard, as it has always been, because simply getting along with one another has always been, and will continue to be, humanity's greatest challenge.

Epilogue: Putting Your Time, Talents, and Treasure to Work (for Others)

> I say you really ought to do what you like to do, not
> what you think you should, because if you're going to
> make a difference in [development] work, it takes decades
> ... [Y]ou need staff, stuff, space, and systems, and that
> requires contributions from many fields, from architecture
> to management. You're part of a big and diverse team ...
> Most of all you need persistence ... Do the kind of things
> you want to do and don't try to imitate someone else's
> plan.
>
> *Paul Farmer, Co-Founder, Partners in Health*[1]

It's become an internet meme, but in many respects it's hard
to give better career or personal advice than that contained
in the precepts of what the Japanese call *ikigai*: seek to be at
the intersection of what the world needs, what you're good
at, what you can get paid for, and what you love doing.
Given the way in which international development has been
framed in this book – as a historical process and an intentional effort to transform societies, polities, economies, and
public administration; and as a "field" populated by a vast
assortment of actors doing different things in different ways
for different reasons – there are surely many entry points for
those wanting to offer up what they have "to make the world
a better place." But no matter which door one enters through
or how long one plans on journeying, it helps to have a map
of the development terrain, to know where that map comes

from, why it looks the way it does, and what the key actors in this space do well and not so well. All of this can help one direct one's energies more adeptly and set reasonable expectations for what can actually be accomplished.

To give more specific and potentially useful advice, however, it helps to go back to the three "developments" – national, big, and small – we have discussed across this book, and map them onto what I will describe as three corresponding types of work that can be done in each of them. These three types of work, I suggest, can be defined by the extent to which they (a) fill space, (b) protect space, or (c) connect space. That might initially sound rather abstract, but with some explanation I hope it will become clear. I describe each of these types below, in order, as well as why they are distinctive yet complementary. I hope you can recognize what you do, or might do, somewhere in these three. No doubt there are some overlaps between them, but for present purposes I think it is helpful to provide a brief analytical framework that will make the distinctions apparent. This framing of different skills and sensibilities in development is grounded in both my lived professional experience and my understanding of how and why the claims made by different groups – in general, not just in development – are so often discordant with those of others.

Each of us are members of different groups – professional associations, community groups, faith-based organizations, political parties, clubs of one kind or another. By design, every such group shares similar interests, commitments, and values, and has a basis on which it makes key decisions. A fruitful analytical distinction between such groups can be made simply on the basis of what each group counts as a question and what it counts as an answer. It is for this reason, for example, that anthropologists and economists rarely attend the same seminar on development: there might be some token recognition, even appreciation, of what the other group does, but each would find the other's topics, language, methods, and modes of reasoning almost entirely unintelligible, uninteresting, and unpersuasive. (Disciplines discipline; they are defined by theory and method.) Similarly, a theological discussion between a Hindu, an evangelical Protestant, and an atheist; a discussion of rights and responsibilities between a libertarian, a communitarian, and a communist; or a conversation about stars between an astrophysicist and an astrologer, are unlikely to get very far. These may be extreme examples, but it is not hard to find lesser versions of them everywhere, especially in the world of development – for example, around what "land" is: how it should be used, by whom, for what, and whether it's even conceivable that it can be "owned" or "sold" (Winchester 2021; Kaneko et al. 2022). In such instances, the struggle to communicate is not because the parties in question are being unreasonable, speak another language, or because they happen to have different perspectives, interests, or incentives which make an accommodation or compromise difficult to forge (though perhaps they do). They are instead members of what sociologists call different "epistemic communities": groups for whom there are fundamental (ontological) differences between, as I said, what counts as a question and what counts as an answer. Hold that distinction for a while (see Figure E.1).

Within each of these groups, it is common to make different kinds of knowledge claims, but for present purposes I'll just

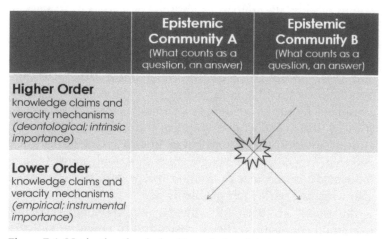

	Epistemic Community A (What counts as a question, an answer)	Epistemic Community B (What counts as a question, an answer)
Higher Order knowledge claims and veracity mechanisms (*deontological; intrinsic importance*)		
Lower Order knowledge claims and veracity mechanisms (*empirical; instrumental importance*)		

Figure E.1 Navigating the clash of knowledge-claiming systems

distinguish between what I call "higher-order" and "lower-order" claims. Lower-order claims are empirical; they can, in principle if not always in practice, be readily verified and thus can be amended, updated, or discarded (again in principle) on the basis of compelling rival claims made within the same level. Higher-order knowledge claims are grounded in non-empirical, ideological, theological, moral, or aspirational values – and are no less powerful or compelling for being so.[2] Any professional seminar is thus mostly a gathering of those with a shared understanding of what counts as a question and what counts as an answer, debating the merits of a particular lower-order knowledge claim: Is growth good for the poor? Do conditional cash transfers work? Does raising the minimum wage help or hinder the working class? When do women's empowerment programs lead to rising rates of domestic violence? The tone of the debates might seem ugly at times, but they are basically "family fights," wherein, as Henry Kissinger famously remarked, the voices are so vicious because the stakes are so small. Engaging with such questions, answers, inferences, and conclusions constitutes the activity of normal social science as most readers of this book would understand that term, but within the framing I've provided here it would also characterize a mid-week discussion among parishioners in Auckland concerned about ways to stem falling weekly attendance at church, or between farmers in rural Mali seeking ways to enhance their crop yields. Such activity, I argue, can be described as "filling a space": one deploys one's training and experience to help solve a known and shared problem (a question), in due course providing a sufficiently credible and legitimate solution (an answer), as judged by other occupants of this "space." It should be stressed that a vast array of important problems in the world, and in development in particular, fit this characterization – and that, crucially, one can gainfully and nobly contribute to the world's betterment by joining forces with those who are also wrestling with such problems.

But things get decidedly messier – provoking everything from mild confusion to deep frustration to potential violence – when different kinds of claims are being made by people from different kinds of groups; that is, when one epistemic community encounters a qualitatively different one (i.e., a group with a very different understanding of what counts as a question and what counts as an answer), and/or when this community is functioning at a higher/lower level of knowledge claiming. Consider, for example, that most people with religious convictions engage in regular acts of prayer, wherein they seek God's (or the gods', or some Higher Power's) comfort, healing, or guidance, doing so because they regard this as right and proper behavior, believing that prayer works (albeit perhaps in mysterious and unexpected ways). This is a quintessential higher-order knowledge claim that is made or invoked every day by billions of people, as it has been for tens of thousands of years: its truth, falsity, or efficacy is entirely immune to whatever "scientific" evidence – i.e., the methods of lower-order knowledge claiming – might be marshalled to support or refute it. The Pope will never publish a paper in which he seeks to demonstrate the power of petitionary prayer by subjecting it to an experiment; and neither should he. Similarly, he would be entirely unmoved by the findings of any of the numerous "studies" claiming to have demonstrated that petitionary prayer does or doesn't work,[3] precisely because he recognizes, along with most people of faith, that these are fundamentally different modes of reasoning and experience, ones that – in principle if not always in practice – can co-exist quite fruitfully if one recognizes the different kinds of questions and answers that higher- and lower-order knowledge-claiming invokes (see Hughes 2012). On the other hand, the Pope (or an imam, a swami, a guru, or a rabbi) might be quite interested in an empirical study rigorously assessing the efficacy of different strategies for increasing members' financial contributions to their local house of worship – because such questions and answers reside quite happily in the lower-order knowledge-claiming domain.

In all three kinds of development discussed in this book, needing to engage constructively across lower- and higher-order knowledge claiming – that is, "connecting *across* (very different kinds of) space" – will be a frequent occurrence, particularly if you find yourself on the front lines of work in health, agriculture, justice, or education. Why these four? Because every group everywhere has a prevailing way of understanding why illness occurs, why the crops fail (or thrive), how order should be maintained, and how (and what) the rising generation should be taught. The foundations of those explanations and understandings will likely reside in a space that can span the full spectrum of lower- and higher-order knowledge claiming. And into that space you, as a "development person," will likely arrive with a rather particular – but unwittingly much narrower – understanding of how the world works, and how others *should* understand how the world works if their lives are to "improve." Learning how to respectfully enter and exit different kinds of lower- and higher-order knowledge-claiming spaces is essential if one is to both "give *and* receive"[4] in the development business.

We've discussed (and distinguished between) development work that "fills space" and development work that "connects space." That leaves the final category – "creating and protecting space" – which is perhaps the most difficult, thankless, and perilous of all, because it entails finding entirely new ways to forge a durable agreement, in relation to problems that have no known (or readily knowable) solution, between groups with fundamentally different understandings of what counts as a question and what counts as an answer, where the interests and objectives of one group can seemingly only be met at another group's direct expense. This is the world of negotiation and diplomacy, where the space for finding shared rules for agreeing (enough) on what the problem is has to be established and consolidated before any solution can even be conceived, let alone articulated, endorsed, funded, and implemented. Years of diligent, unglamorous work can unravel in a moment; failure can lead to thousands of deaths; yet success can sometimes still be achieved.[5]

The importance and distinctive nature of work that creates and protects space becomes clear when it is contrasted with work that fills space, because rather different forms of expertise are needed in each. Halfway through the class I teach at Harvard Kennedy School, I give a lecture on what it means to be a "development expert" – I now have enough grey hair and professional visibility to often have that awkward title bestowed upon me, but while I like to think I have come to know a little about development processes, and probably know more now than I did twenty-five years ago, "development expert" is a label I try to wear lightly, if I must wear it at all. In that lecture, I stress that technical expertise is real but rare, its application is deeply necessary and consequential, and for certain kinds of development problems it is exactly what is needed. For other kinds of development problems, however – and certainly the bulk of those associated with building state capability for policy implementation – routinely prioritizing the singular deployment of a narrow form of technical expertise as the optimal solution is itself part of the problem (Pritchett and Woolcock 2004).

As noted above, my preferred metaphorical, ideal-type juxtaposition is between expertise that fills space, expertise that connects space, and expertise that creates and protects space. The distinction between filling and protecting space roughly corresponds to, respectively, Theory X and Theory Y in the management literature (as famously articulated by McGregor 1960): Theory X assumes that workers are passive slackers, thereby requiring close supervision and monitoring in order for organizations to function at a high and sustained level; Theory Y advocates giving workers more expansive discretion and autonomy, on the assumption that they will be more productive, motivated, and fulfilled when they are creatively solving problems rather than merely adhering to fixed rules and requirements.

I like the Theory X/Y distinction expressed in the terms of "filling" versus "protecting" space because it broadly reflects the different skills and sensibilities that, to me, are so readily on display in development decision-making – whether in the boardroom, the online seminar, the policy forum, the diplomatic table, or the village meeting hall. The space-fillers primarily perceive their job, and their kindred colleagues' job, as one of controlling (empirically, epistemologically, managerially) the extraneous "noisy" factors intruding on the space they've carefully identified so that, into this space, their particular, somewhere-verified solution can be deftly but decisively inserted. It's what Atul Gawande (2017) calls the "savior doctor" model, in which one provides "a definitive intervention at a critical moment ... with a clear, calculable, frequently transformative outcome." I've checked the key indicators ("vital signs"), asked my go-to questions, diligently eliminated various possibilities; I've scanned the decision-tree as I understand it, and determined that the highest-probability solution to this problem is X. The faster and more "cleanly" I can do this, the more genuinely "expert" (efficient and effective) I believe myself to be. Providing such decisive input into this space is emotionally thrilling; it vindicates all my years of elite education and hard work, pays me real money, yields the tantalizing allure of future successes at grander scales with higher stakes, and bestows upon me tangible professional accolades and high social status. Like nature, I abhor a vacuum, so I've confidently stepped in where the less rigorous fear to tread. I'm trained and socialized to think counterfactually, so I can't help but indulge my vainglorious *ceteris paribus* fantasy that, but for my presence at that moment, things would have turned out so differently ... Heck, I've changed history!

To be clear: if it's your child's life on the line, requiring a serious technical diagnosis and medical response, you would do whatever it takes to get that expertise; delivering that expertise under "stress test" pressure is itself a crucial skill (Geithner 2014); vital stuff happens in "the room where it happened." And, if we're honest, most of us quite like being in that room. (But, since I've just invoked *Hamilton*, I'll add that I think an under-appreciated virtue of that wonderful musical is its recognition that, as Wilkinson (2020) puts it, "After you've turned the world upside down, you have to figure out what comes next. You have to figure out your laws, your economy, your foreign policy. You also have to figure out who matters, who makes the rules, and – maybe most importantly – who tells the story. Every culture war is about who gets to define the terms and control the narrative, and that's no different now than it was in 2016 or 1812 or 1776.")

The skills and sensibilities of Theory Y (or "Route Y," as Honig [forthcoming] cleverly calls its applications in development practice) are very different but equally necessary when it comes to creating and protecting space for informed, inclusive deliberation; promoting more equitable contests; and enabling good struggles. In this space, infused with and guided by some minimally but locally legitimate processes, parties seek to find, implement, and uphold specific solutions to the complex challenges associated with wrenching social change, bridging wide disagreement, negotiating reasonable differences, and resolving divisive dissent. Call it the "faithful social worker" model (full disclosure – my mother and one of my sisters were social workers): I may have seen versions of this vexing problem before, but ultimately each one is different in ways neither I nor (most likely) anyone else can or could fully anticipate; if there's any decision-tree (or trees?), it's one I've painstakingly assembled on the basis of hard-won experience and yet it may be quite different from that of others. For example, I can only hope that my decision to remove these kids from their family – one I've deemed sufficiently "dysfunctional" – is somehow going to be better for all of them; but even if this particular intervention "works" in the short-run I don't really know what the long-term outcomes for them will be. Making and enacting such decisions is deeply contingent and emotionally fraught – at best I've made a horrible situation slightly less horrible; at worst I've amplified and perpetuated the awfulness. At the outset, it's not clear which outcome will prevail, what timeframe or trajectory it will take to get there, and what collateral effects it will generate along the way. There is no clear counterfactual. My education gave me a few useful professional principles to guide my actions and helped me understand the legal/administrative terrain I was about to enter, but nothing could truly simulate or anticipate the complexity, uncertainty, idiosyncrasy, and paralyzing stress associated with each case I find myself addressing. For doing and dealing with all this, I get paid a pittance; few accord me any serious professional respect (whether neighbors, random strangers I meet on airplanes, or old friends at high-school reunions). I get the blame if outcomes "fail" but no credit if they "succeed"; my efforts mostly feel like that of a garden hose confronting an inferno; "lessons learned" are never actually learned by the organizations I work for; and if I move to another state, let alone another country, my knowledge and certifications will have to be acquired all over again. So I'm stuck; I do my best "here," but no one else "there" really knows or cares.

People way braver, stronger, and more persistent than me sign up for entire careers that often look and feel like this latter world (e.g., middle-school teachers, inner-city police officers, youth workers, in-home nursing assistants); much development work, I suggest, also looks a lot like this. Of course, we need all three of these approaches – skills and sensibilities that fill space (Route X), that connect across space (Route Y), and that create/protect space (call it Route Z!)[6] – and various combinations thereof. Alas, in development, our prevailing high-modern administrative systems, political imperatives, professional structures, and career incentives are just deeply stacked in favor of doing X over Y and Z.[7] These administrative proclivities are now reinforced by the dominance of methodological approaches seeking or providing ready-made, narrowly verified "solutions" (no matter how niche or small), whose seductive overtures only have ever-greater traction in a world in which the once-broad policy objective of *national* development has, in the aftermath of the Cold War, been steadily weakened geopolitically or deemed passé, overtaken by advocacy for particular causes or particular people offering more direct, targeted, and emotionally compelling programs (what I have called "small development"), sometimes explicitly doing so because they deem "foreign aid" to have failed.

What to do? Those championing development practices that seek to connect and protect space, such as proponents of Problem-Driven Iterative Adaptation (discussed in Chapter 4), need to deploy combinations of X, Y, and Z approaches if they are to create and protect the space for development generally, and for state capability efforts in particular. If you sign up for a career in any form of development work, however, you should be under no illusions about how long, hard, and uncertain this work will be, and recognize that *everyone* in development needs to somehow create a space for valuing, cultivating, protecting, and integrating very different forms of "expertise" (Eyal 2019). (And for supporting the boring, unseen work of prevention as much as the more visibly spectacular work of cure; see Clarke and Dercon 2016.) In the solution space for responding to complex development problems, perpetuating monopolies that decide what counts as a question and what counts as an answer is as insidiously counterproductive as it is in markets for goods and services.

But most people have no desire to spend a career working in development, at least in its big or small forms; perhaps a few more choose to promote their country's national development by committing to a career (or stint) in public service. Even so, this book has been written on the premise that many more (perhaps most) people want to help "make the world a better place" by contributing some measure of their particular talents, time, and treasure (money). *Everyone* has something to give, no matter how seemingly insignificant or obscure, but as the opening reflection from Paul Farmer reminds us, that something needs to be connected to others, to the "staff, stuff, space, and systems" that can put it to work. No matter what your motivation, I hope these decisions about how to contribute – at least as they pertain to international development – can now be more informed ones, the reader having (hopefully) learned something about how the "aid industry" is structured, how it came to be that way, what it seeks to do, why it struggles with certain kinds of key problems, and where improvements need to be sought if the world is to ever achieve, let alone by 2030, anything like the pledges it has made to itself in the Sustainable Development Goals. Certain professions – medicine, engineering, education – already have systems in place that make this possible for their members; and programs for young people (such as the Peace Corps in the United States) that give them extended time living in low-income countries during their formative years are vital investments for both "givers" and "receivers." Making generous financial contributions to charities and other small development agencies whose work aligns with your values is always a good thing; just be sure to do your homework on them, as you would when making any other kind of major financial transaction.

As I noted at the outset, the main messages of this book are drawn from four lectures originally given to young British lawyers offering their services pro bono to organizations in lower-income countries with legal development concerns, so I will conclude with the advice I gave to them – and by extension, give to anyone with talents, time, and treasure they wish to offer up for the benefit of others.

First, in making any contribution, it helps to have an informed sense of the big picture: of where the organization you will partner with sits in the larger landscape of national, big, and small development agencies, and of what counts as a question (or "problem") for this organization and what counts as an answer (or "solution" or "success") – because it is highly likely that other organizations (their competitors, opponents, or partners) will have rather different understandings of these issues.

Second, understand that it is also highly likely that how you were trained to do your version of this work, and the skills for which you are now likely paid relatively handsomely, will overlap only partially with what is required in the situation in which you will likely find yourself. That's OK; it's just that you're used to filling space, so be patient with yourself (and others) as you figure out how to connect, create, and protect space for others – especially political space wherein locally legitimate solutions can be forged and sustained.

Third, it helps to have a sense of how, historically, effective change (e.g., political, medical, educational, financial, or any other kind of reform) happened. It may have been due in part to the work of diligent professionals, but for the hardest challenges (e.g., justice, inclusion, gender equality) it was probably also because brave teams and broad social movements made long-term commitments and endured many deep disappointments and setbacks along the way. This process can be enhanced by advocating for international development via your own domestic political systems.

Fourth, don't see yourself as development's version of Gawande's "savior doctor" (even if you do actually end up saving lives): you can only do what you do because hundreds of others are doing what they do, probably with vastly less recognition, appreciation, or remuneration. And even if you feel overwhelmed much of the time, as you probably will, it's important to appreciate that others have it far worse. As a famous professional football coach in Australia once memorably said, when asked on the eve of a major game how he was dealing with all the pressure: "Stress is not being able to feed your kids."

Which is to say, fifth, put your problems – and your achievements, for that matter – in perspective; for millions of people, every day is consumed by worrying about how they can possibly feed, house, and protect their precious children. On a good day, the wonders of "development" ease that burden just a little; on an even better day, they make poverty and insecurity history. It is our good fortune to live in a moment when, for the first time, achieving this is actually possible; the price of this possibility, however, is assuming responsibility for saving us from ourselves: from our endless capacity to sow division, to destroy each other, and the planet. As the opening epigraph from Paul Virilio starkly reminds us, the invention of the ship was indeed also the invention of the shipwreck.

We live in a deeply interdependent world, in which few of us now have any direct connection to securing the basic essentials of life. Unlike any of the preceding 2,500 genera-tions of humans, most of us don't grow our own food, collect our own water, dispose of our own waste, make our own clothes, build our own houses, supply our own energy, or protect our own communities. Others do these things for us; in exchange, we offer up our particular skills and resources, and we exchange (trade) with one another. Doing this more fairly and equitably, at scale, *is* the wonder of development. Whether seeking a full-time career in the development business, committing one's spare time to causes of concern, or just seeking to be more informed about global affairs, it is this recognition of our deep interdependence, and our gratitude to those around us and those who went before us, that should inspire us to give back, to offer up, to pay forward.

Notes

Prelude

1 The historical instantiation and inherent contention associated with the ideas of "progress" and "improvement," in both the moral and material senses, are explored in chapter 1.

2 An indicative empirical example of such phenomena is provided by Berry (2015), who examines the complex ways in which seemingly successful efforts in Rwanda to empower women (e.g., Rwanda has the world's highest percentage of women in parliament) has been "undermined by deeply rooted social processes" (p. 1) elicited by this apparent success. Hessler (2022) provides a firsthand account of the ways in which rapid and sustained economic growth in rural China over the last two decades has created wide (sometimes perplexingly different) intergenerational life experiences: parents remain poor illiterate rural farmers even as their children reside in the urban middle class attending university and driving electric cars. More formally, see also Ang (2016).

3 Pitts (2005) deftly explores the emergence of different arguments used to justify these practices. See also Armitage (2012).

4 See, among others, Szreter (1997); on associated processes of widening inequality during the British Industrial Revolution, see Allen (2009). Scott (2017) summarizes recent evidence indicating that the emergence of the world's first cities and "civilizations" (i.e., antiquity's earliest states) left vast swathes of the population worse off.

5 Encapsulated in the classic article by Romer (1993).

6 See Pritchett and Woolcock (2004).

7 On this point, see Adichie's (2009) famous "The danger of a

single story" TED talk address, observed over 31 million times. Even so, there is an equivalent "danger" in having no story, or too many competing stories.

8 See chapter 1 of Klitgaard (1990).
9 I take this to be the central critique of Giridharadas (2019). However, by arguing – as I do – that development derives its legitimacy and content from incorporating everyone, there must, by definition, be a role for those deemed to be "elites." I address such matters in the epilogue.
10 And by virtue of my career-long residence outside academic departments of sociology, I strongly suspect I'm now widely regarded as being neither "in" nor "of" the world of sociology! Such is my life.

1 Navigating Our Diverging, Integrated World

1 See Ruth Maclean and Caleb Kabanda, "What do the protectors of Congo's peatlands get in return?," *New York Times*, February 21, 2002, at https://www.nytimes.com/interactive/2022/02/21/headway/peatlands-congo-climate-change.html.
2 Unsurprisingly, "development" has several different meanings and connotations in other languages – which I delight in exploring each year in the opening week of my class at Harvard Kennedy School. For example, see Heryanto (1988) for an insightful discussion on "the development of development" in Bahasa Indonesian.
3 The Sustainable Development Goals will be referred to at several points in this book. They are the seventeen development targets, set in 2015, to be achieved in rich and poor countries alike by 2030. Overseen by the United Nations, they are the product of extensive global deliberation.
4 The United States Agency for International Development (USAID) is one arm of the US government's foreign policy apparatus; in Sweden the equivalent agency is called the Swedish International Development Cooperation Agency (Sida), presided over by a minister with cabinet status; in the UK, it is called the Foreign, Commonwealth and Development Office (FCDO). For a brief shining moment in the early 2000s there were about a dozen OECD countries that had granted independent ministerial and cabinet status to international development. That the number is now only four (Canada,

Ireland, Sweden, and Norway) – many once-independent agencies having been subsumed back into ministries of foreign affairs, from whence they had come – says a lot about the more insular and instrumental focus of the wealthy nations in recent years.

5 Placing it in the same rhetorical space that Americans use when they talk about Big Business, Big Pharma, Big Government, etc.

6 I've named this aspect after the eponymous development text *Small is Beautiful* (Schumacher 1973). That said, I am conscious that others have used the big/small development distinction in somewhat different ways (e.g., Hart 2001; Lewis 2019), where "big" development refers to intentional policy initiatives and "small" development to the human-centered outcomes emanating from them (see also Cohen and Shenton 1996). The distinctions I've drawn on this point – which I've deployed publicly for over a decade (see Woolcock 2012) – center on the different unit of analysis (countries, individuals) at which the focus of attention and action is directed, not the size of the organizations involved. (In Bangladesh, for example, the non-government organization BRAC has some 100,000 employees – more than six times bigger than the World Bank – yet primarily focuses its activities at the local level on the "extreme poor"; see Matin 2022.) The difference between "big" and "small" development is vast, both substantively (the scale and consequences of action) and politically (the influence wielded by the actors involved in it), even as small development efforts in recent years have assumed and asserted greater importance (e.g., in academia, by those declaring the big development questions – such as "the effectiveness of foreign aid" – to be largely empirically unanswerable, electing instead to address small-scale interventions via randomized controlled trials). As I hope my distinction between national development and big development also makes clear, I think it's important to distinguish analytically between the everyday socio-economic activities undertaken (or overseen) by sovereign national governments and those enabled, constrained, or imposed by external agencies working in partnership with those governments – again for substantive reasons (the nature and extent of these partnerships can range from mutually fruitful to deeply dysfunctional) and political reasons (this is a key juncture at which pressure is leveraged by citizens, corporations, governments, and aid agencies alike). I hope it goes without saying

that, in certain large countries, the spirit (if not the letter) of national development encompasses the work of constituent states/provinces (several of which in India and China, for example, would be among the world's most populous countries were they to secede) and major cities (for similar reasons).

7 Different forms of national development, as manifest in the capabilities of state administration and the nature of state–society relations, can also help explain variations between North and South Vietnam over this time period (see Dell et al. 2018).

8 Source: Our World in Data; World Bank (2020e).

9 The data in this figure reflect the relationship between levels of economic development (in median income or consumption) and the incidence of extreme poverty across many years of data collection; they have been standardized for broad comparative purposes by using a common 2011 measure of purchasing power parity (PPP).

10 In 2010, Egypt had an extreme poverty rate less than 2 percent but a median per capita consumption of around $1,600.

11 In 2002, Bolivia had an extreme poverty rate of 24.6 percent and a median per capita income of $1,579. In other words, with roughly the same level of national wealth as Egypt (circa 2010), Bolivia's rate of extreme poverty was at least ten times higher.

12 As a result of the decade-long war in Syria (and its effects on the Mashreq region more generally), poverty is estimated to have risen by 7.1 percent in Lebanon and by 6 percent in Iraq (World Bank 2020a).

13 In 2014, Panama had an extreme poverty rate of 3.51 percent but a median per capita income of over $5,100. Panama was thus roughly three times richer than Egypt but had twice as many people living in extreme poverty.

14 On the practical challenges of distinguishing between different levels of extreme poverty, see the compelling photographic project "One Hundred Homes" (https://onehundredhomes.in), which visually presents 100 households corresponding to each centile of the income distribution in India (i.e., the poorest 1 percent to the richest 1 percent). Among other things, the project asks viewers to nominate which of two pairs of households is "poorer" – e.g., one household deemed to be at the 5 percent level of income and another at 15 percent level, though such information is of course withheld until the viewer makes

their choice. That such choices turn out to be so hard to make is precisely the point.

15 More formally, scholars have termed this an aspiration for a society characterized by a "benign sociology" (Bayly 2011: 50) in which a person's "morally irrelevant characteristics" such as race, religion, gender, disability, and sexual orientation no longer become "systematic sources of social disadvantage" (Sunstein 1993: 259). Under different circumstances – the case of college admissions, for example, where administrators may explicitly seek demographic and geographic diversity – such characteristics may well become "morally relevant."

16 Invoking the concept of a social contract as the analytical basis on which to discuss state–society relations and the politics of inclusion/exclusion has a long and varied history. In contemporary development discourse, and especially in debates surrounding social protection programs, it has invoked both liberal (interest-based, utilitarian) and social (protecting rights, promoting justice) justifications, the logics of which give rise to rather different approaches to policy and practice (Hickey 2011). The term "social contract" is often used synonymously with related concepts such as "social compact," "social cohesion," "social capital," and "political settlement" (Khan 2018). For present purposes, our concern is with promoting the spirit rather than the specific letter of these terms; emergent tensions (linguistic, substantive) associated with deploying one discourse rather than another are best resolved through prevailing deliberative forums in each country context.

17 See also BTI (2020), which reports that each year since 2009 there has been, in the 129 countries they track, "a series of accelerating trends that are halting the progress of democracy and threatening to bolster regressive tendencies." Even so, "many governments are facing increasingly determined citizens and resilient institutions that are no longer willing to tolerate social inequality, mismanagement and corruption, and which are finding new strategies to keep up the pressure."

18 On the steadily rising approval and practice of inter-racial marriage in the US over the last fifty years, see *The Economist* (2017); on the rising sense among the lowest castes in India of their growing equality with higher castes, see Kapur et al. (2010); on "the steady movement towards gender parity for more than 25 years" in school enrollment and basic literacy, see UNESCO (2019: 12) – though on workplace relations, "after

decades of improvement, progress for women … has stalled in recent years" (*The Economist* 2019); on the steadily rising health coverage and education access of those with disabilities in Latin America and the Caribbean, especially Chile and Costa Rica, see World Bank (2020d). To be sure, there is wide variation around these general trends – including some recent reversals, many of them deeply disconcerting – but over time, social equality laws, norms, and practices have steadily (if fitfully, painstakingly, precariously, unevenly, and incompletely) improved.

19 Though here too there is variation; see the most recent work of the EU's Anti-Corruption Monitor (https://www .againstcorruption.eu).

20 The analytical foundations of, and practical actions associated with, possible "new approaches" to building state capability are outlined in Andrews et al. (2017).

21 See also the catalogue of research findings on the parlous state of learning in developing countries produced by the Research on Improving Systems of Education (RISE) program (https:// riseprogramme.org).

22 A corresponding argument can be made for multilateralism, which in principle enables the world's countries to engage with one another on the basis of shared rules rather than a patchwork of idiosyncratic, bilateral deals.

23 Of course, drastically lowering transactions costs to exchange and movement can also enable the spread of "bads" as well as "goods," as the global experience with Covid-19 tragically demonstrates. Similarly, it has long been recognized (since at least Schumpeter's emphasis in the 1930s that economic growth was a wrenching process of "creative destruction") that the "social trust" characterizing a certain level of development may change (even decline) as economic growth alters, for example with rates of urbanization driving rural residents from "stable" village life into "chaotic" cities. The very configuration of social life, as measured by its social networks (Jackson 2019), is altered by economic growth.

24 See also Raimondo (2019) for a summary of how the World Bank is applying social contract diagnostics in its operational work, especially in the Middle East and North Africa region.

25 See https://endhomelessness.org/homelessness-in-america /homelessness-statistics/state-of-homelessness-report, citing data from the US government's Department of Housing and Urban Development.

26 See also Kristof and WuDunn (2020).
27 See also https://www.nytimes.com/interactive/2020/06/04 /opinion/coronavirus-health-race-inequality.html.
28 In 2002, Kyrgyz Republic had a poverty rate of 2.54 percent and a median consumption of $1,581 (PPP 2011).
29 In 2015, Bulgaria had an extreme poverty rate of 3.02 percent and a median consumption of $5,240 (PPP 2011).
30 In addition to these "political failure" scenarios, which are roughly analogous to more familiar "market failure" conditions, the potential of sound development policies can also struggle to be realized because of (what might be called) "civil society failure" (see Mansuri and Rao 2012) – the inability of social groups to cooperate and coordinate, to overcome collective action problems (e.g., management of common-pool resources, such as water), to serve as a necessary countervailing force on states and firms.
31 Kleinfeld (2018) finds, for example, that most of the cases she examined where peace settlements were reached after extended violent conflict entailed giving prominent posts in the new administration to leaders of former rebel groups, many of whom were widely known to have committed war crimes. This is an instance where adopting policy based on "the evidence" leads into spaces that are, from an ethical and moral perspective, deeply fraught.
32 Indeed, even or especially when development *succeeds*, Huntington argued, it serves to "extend political consciousness, multiply political demands, [and] broaden political participation. [But in doing so] these changes undermine traditional sources of political authority and traditional political institutions; they enormously complicate the problems of creating new bases of political association and new political institutions combining legitimacy and effectiveness. The rates of social mobilization and the expansion of political participation are high; the rates of political organization and institutionalization are low. The result is political instability and disorder" (1968: 5).
33 On the implications of legal pluralism for development policy, see Tamanaha et al. (2012). See also Benton (2002).
34 Challenges needing to be addressed include (a) responding to the uncomfortable findings outlined in Kleinfeld (2018), which are that a common element of peace settlements forged in the aftermath of extended violence is the granting of considerable

political power and financial resources to former warlords (who, in a better world, would be answering for their crimes against humanity in the International Criminal Court); and (b) recognizing that efforts over many decades to promote "capacity building" have regularly yielded deeply disappointing outcomes (Andrews 2013; on the specific case of Malawi, see Bridges and Woolcock 2017).

35 Drawing on comprehensive data and deploying sophisticated methodological analyses, researchers have been able to demonstrate numerous ways in which the institutional legacies of colonialism endure to the present. Contemporary development outcomes and social trust in Africa, for example, are weakest where the extraction of slaves between 1400 and 1900 was most intense (Nunn 2008; Nunn and Wantchekon 2011); indeed, Nunn goes so far as to conclude that "Africa's slave trades account for *all* of Africa's poor performance relative to other developing countries" (2020: 1442, emphasis added). Similarly, development outcomes in Peru are significantly lower today where the Spanish set up forced labor systems between 1573 and 1812 (Dell 2010); the type of legal system (common or civil law: "common law stands for the strategy of social control that seeks to support private market outcomes, whereas civil law seeks to replace such outcomes with state-desired allocations") imposed by colonists has had significantly different effects on how well private property (especially when held by outside investors) was secured and exchanged (La Porta et al. 2008: 286); the prevalence of certain disease vectors in particular places shaped whether colonialists constructed "extractive" or "inclusive" institutions (Acemoglu et al. 2001); overt resistance today to "western" medicine, such as vaccines, has been traced to earlier episodes of longstanding medical malpractice (Lowes and Montero 2017); and land tenure arrangements (*zamindar*) introduced by the British Raj into particular areas of Bengal continue to shape public investment to this day, with development expenditures as a proportion of total revenues under such systems some 70 percent lower seven decades after colonialism ended (Banerjee and Iyer 2005). Importantly for our purposes, more recent work by Lee suggests that the mechanism by which *zamindar*-type land tenure systems lowered development outcomes was not the system itself but weakened state capacity in the districts where they were located; such districts have "a strong and consistent

positive association with 20th-century economic activity" (Lee 2019: 412).

36   The classic work of Bates (1981), for example, argued that in their quest to be "modern," many African countries had rushed to industrialization but in the process heavily distorted markets in food (cheap prices in urban areas to placate potential/actual unrest), agricultural production (large, high-modern farms privileging elites who could afford them), and consumer goods (inefficient monopolies in inputs and products).

37   The broader critique of international development agencies as "anti-politics machines" (Ferguson 1990; see also Escobar 1995) rests on two additional arguments, namely that (a) in wanting to appear and be "apolitical" (which a certain reading of their articles of association requires them to be) they ignore their own role as – and thereby absolve themselves of the responsibilities and liabilities associated with being – key political players in national and regional politics; and that (b) agencies frame development problems in client countries in ways that comport with the particular "solutions" (projects and policy advice) they happen to wield or favor, irrespective of whether these are the actual problems confronting the country (or in fact stem from the adoption of these favored projects and policies). This leads inexorably to a conclusion that development has "failed." A response to these critiques, however, needs to begin with recognizing that seeking to be apolitical can be a virtue if an agency can maintain a credible stance as a neutral arbiter, independent advisor, or, if necessary, a beacon of countervailing power (e.g., bringing to light clear human rights or environmental abuses); that projects and policy advice have their place as legitimate instruments of enhanced human welfare; and that managing a modern state in an interconnected world, and meeting the global development goals to which 193 sovereign governments have committed themselves, must necessarily entail the use of modern administrative tools, technologies, and professional standards. It's hard to conclude that development has "failed" when global poverty levels have never been lower in recorded human history (see also Rosling 2018). Even so, as we discuss below, in the early twenty-first century greater space can and must be accorded for taking politics seriously in development debates.

38   In both these cases, of course, events were also powerfully shaped by major geopolitical entanglements.

39 Such an argument was mournfully expressed long before the post-World War II "development era." Ki Hajar Dewantara, an education reformer in Indonesia, lamented in the mid-1930s: "How often we have been misled by presumed needs which we considered natural but which we later realized were proper to alien forms of civilization ... We have added much new cultural material, the value of which cannot be discounted; however, it often fits so ill with our own style or is so far removed from it that we can use it at best as a decoration and not as material to build with. It is quite understandable why we have been so mistaken in our choice. In the first place, much has to be chosen, and there has been so little to choose from" (as cited in Harper 2011: 193).

2 Managing a Contentious World

1 This section refines and extends sections from Woolcock (2017).
2 Popular summaries of this rapidly expanding literature can be found in Davis (2009), Fukuyama (2011), Reich (2018), and Galor (2022).
3 While Australia was settled some 60,000 years ago, humans did not arrive in New Zealand until around 1300.
4 Some scholars have argued that Biblical warrant for "subduing the Earth" was found in Genesis 1:28; others have stressed that the original Hebrew word (*rada*) was not synonymous with "domination" (instead being more akin to "tilling"), while Harrison (1999) argues that "stewardship" should be given equal if not greater emphasis as a complementary term.
5 The fascinating (if tumultuous) history of the *idea* of "progress" is outlined in Nisbet (1980), Lasch (1991), and Wagner (2016); see also Slack (2015) on the invention of the related idea of "improvement," and Palmer (2017). Khālidī (1981) provides an intellectual history of "progress" in classical Islam.
6 Slack argues that the very word "improvement" was invented by the English, and that in the seventeenth century it had no counterpart in any other European language. Strategically, "improvement" came to occupy a distinctive space among rival approaches to betterment, such as "revolution" and "reformation," with its focus on "gradual, piecemeal but cumulative" change (Slack 2015: 1).
7 What the British subsequently did with their extraordinary

wealth, transportation systems, and military might – i.e., create a global empire on which "the sun never set," much of it made possible because of slavery, the devastating effects of which endure to this day (Nunn 2020) – is another story. For present purposes, we must acknowledge that virtually every country, upon becoming more economically prosperous, has invested heavily in its military and explicitly sought to expand its regional (if not global) geopolitical influence. It is not hard to conclude that a world "free of poverty" will also be a world awash in nuclear weapons.

8 See Pomeranz (2001) on why, for example, China's numerous pioneering technological inventions did not lead to broad-based prosperity and territorial expansion, but rather, over time, to a "great divergence" from Europe's rising standards of living.

9 The origins, mechanisms, durability, and impact of the Elizabethan Poor Law – and its weaker successor, the New Poor Law, unveiled in the early nineteenth century – have long been studied by economic and social historians. See important work by Solar (1995), Hindle (2004), Smith (2011), and Slack (2015); for a recent summary, see Cooper and Szreter (2021: Chapter 11), who argue that 400+ years of the Poor Law was the template and inspiration for Britain's post-World War II welfare state.

10 See, for example, Helleiner (2014) and Hathaway and Shapiro (2017).

11 Noting the disruptive nature of social, economic, and political change has a long intellectual pedigree (e.g., in the writings of Edmund Burke), but finds its most detailed contemporary expression in Moore (1965) and Huntington (1968). More recently, see Scott (1998), Bates (2010), Fukuyama (2011), and – at a more micro level in rural Indonesia – Barron et al. (2011).

12 A more colloquial or pragmatic way of expressing this might be to say that where most of the focus in development is on what policies should be adopted, process legitimacy is concerned with how to ensure that the procedures followed to determine policy priorities and their associated implementation modalities align with prevailing understandings of what is considered fair and reasonable, especially by those who are least well placed to respond to the outcomes of policy decisions.

13 Doing so via processes referred to as "legal pluralism" (Tamanaha 2021b), in which multiple forms and sources of "law" (or rules systems more generally) co-exist, with varying

degrees of coherence, power, and shared legitimacy. The classic citation is Merry (1988). This issue is discussed in greater detail below.

14 In the United States, independent groups such as the Stanford-MIT Healthy Elections Project (https://healthyelections.org) exist for precisely this purpose. Needless to say, this group's work has greatly expanded following the 2020 presidential election.

15 See, for example, the gracious concession speech given by George H. W. Bush upon losing the 1992 US presidential election to Bill Clinton; at https://www.youtube.com/watch?v= sMLmaZ8hUwM.

16 Indeed, "the ends don't justify the means" is a widely shared moral principle. One of the earliest (and perhaps innate) moral principles children articulate is their sense of fairness. For a broader review of the forms and importance of legitimacy in public administration, see Suddaby et al. (2017).

17 See Berry (2015) on the socio-political dynamics in Rwanda shaping the paradoxical effects on women of political empowerment, rising education levels, and labor-force participation, where "efforts to remedy women's subordination may actually end up reinforcing it" (p. 1).

18 This type of argument is frequently made by those seeking to "make globalization work" (Rodrik 1999b, Stiglitz 2007); i.e., that for the legitimacy of globalization's many benefits to "winners" to be sustained, policymakers must more assiduously anticipate and redress the difficult costs to "losers" (e.g., unemployment in key industries, potentially leading to the economic decline of entire communities and the alienation of voting blocs). On policy strategies for responding to these challenges, see, among others, Catão and Obstfeld (2019).

19 The films *Even the Rain* (*También La Lluvia*) (2010) and *Crash* (2004) (among many others) deftly capture the conflicts that can ensue when competing/incompatible systems of process legitimacy fester unresolved.

20 A voluminous literature provides varying accounts of how slavery, long regarded as a normal and natural social institution, became, over a long and violent time period, formally outlawed (even as it continues in different forms to this day).

21 A view powerfully articulated in an interview with Albert Hirschman, published in Swedberg (1990; see especially p. 164). The classic paper on this point is Macaulay (1963) on the non-contractual aspects of contracts.

22 This is a slight extension of Kahneman's (2011) famous distinction between "fast" (intuitive, instinctive) and "slow" (patient, deliberative, reflective) thinking. A related idea is Polanyi's (1966) notion of "tacit" knowledge – the repository of insights and skills that cannot be readily codified or even articulated but is nonetheless routinely invoked or called upon to navigate everyday life. Tacit knowledge, when harnessed collectively, can be the basis of innovation (Leonard and Sensiper 1998); its potential to be harnessed collectively, I argue, turns on the extent to which group members accord it legitimacy (whether explicitly or implicitly).

23 And as Rodrik (1999a) and others have argued, sustained long-run economic growth is mostly about managing distributional tensions during crises.

24 The risk of hypocrisy is wide, given that, almost inevitably, there is bound to be a gap between an international agency's or donor country's official proclamations and its lived instantiation. Even an implicit claim that "We recognize that the institutional and policy changes we are asking of you are difficult to achieve, but we did it, and continue to do it, and such changes eventually yield clear material improvements, so you can and should adopt them too," is doomed to disappoint, since detractors only need to find – or inflate or invent – a single instance of inconsistency to impugn the entire venture.

25 For a more detailed discussion of the role of "meta-rules" in local-level conflict mediation and the development process more generally, see Barron et al. (2004).

26 This is essentially how diplomacy is supposed to work: designated agents follow the established (meta-)rules of international law and diplomacy to reach agreements acceptable to both sides.

27 The transition from "deals" to "rules" in development is discussed and empirically assessed in various papers by Pritchett and Hallward-Driemeier (see, for example, Hallward-Driemeier and Pritchett 2015).

28 It should be stressed that such deliberations are inherently precarious and can readily result in one side simply resorting to superior military and/or economic strength in order to have its particular understanding of process legitimacy ("might is right") prevail. Cronon's classic analysis of colonial New England, for example, documents how contending claims between native populations and colonial settlers regarding the appropriate use, ownership, and transfer of "land" was the dynamic underlying

subsequent land-use patterns, settlements, and conflicts. (One only has to visit Plymouth Plantation today to see, most graphically, the vast contrast in how "land" was understood by each group; as Cronon wryly observes, the native populations "thought they were selling one thing... [while] the English thought they were buying another" (1983: 70).) Infamously, so many of the painstakingly negotiated land treaties between native populations and settlers were summarily ignored, only now eliciting the beginnings of public conversations about the legal and moral merits of "reparations" payments for these violations. Needless to say, such debates turn on whose version of what constitutes process legitimacy prevails, and thus what meta-rules can be forged for negotiating the wrenchingly difficult challenge of whether and how to atone "now" for transgressions "then" (but whose effects endure).

29 Notwithstanding that certain groups, over millennia, have overtly and intentionally sought to escape the predations and impositions such "membership" is perceived by them to entail (Scott 2009).

30 To date, the empirical work on process legitimacy (per se), and related terms such as "fairness," has primarily been conducted in the fields of social psychology and law (e.g., most prominently, in the work of Tom Tyler), with only preliminary forays into developing countries. See Levi et al. (2009) for an early effort to measure "legitimizing beliefs," and more recently, the special issue of the *Journal of Intervention and Statebuilding* on assessing "performance-based legitimacy" in "areas of limited statehood" (Levi 2018).

3 Building a Better World

1 A cynical interpretation of the Golden Rule, of course, has long been "Those who have the gold make the rules."

2 In 2015, the world – or, more precisely, 193 countries – formally pledged to meeting, by 2030, a set of seventeen Sustainable Development Goals (SDGs), comprising 157 numerical targets assessed by 232 indicators. (For further details see https://sdgs.un.org/goals.) It's easy to be cynical about the SDGs ("they are so ambitious precisely because no one takes them seriously"), or to dismiss their scale, scope, and ambition as wishful thinking ("there's no way any single country will ever declare itself to have achieved 'effective, accountable and inclusive institutions

at all levels'" [SDG #16], let alone all 193 countries). Even so, they remain eminently noble in their aspiration; they are benchmarks against which the actions of signatory governments can (in principle) be held to account, and are the product of arguably the most intensive and extensive consultation process in human history.

3 The following paragraphs update and refine selected passages from Pritchett et al. (2013).

4 The classic definition here is that of Kuznets (1966), who argued that modern economic growth was a product of enhanced productivity (as opposed to, say, rents from natural resource extraction or theft). Thus, even though the Slovak Republic and Saudi Arabia have roughly comparable levels of per capita wealth, in the former it is a product of modern economic growth ("development"), whereas in the latter it is merely a result of exporting oil.

5 Note that this may or may not manifest itself in a democracy. For present purposes, *modern* polities are polities that reflect the aggregate preferences of the population (whatever those preferences happen to be).

6 That is, rights and opportunities are incrementally afforded to people irrespective of their race, health status, ethnicity, gender, religion, or other social/demographic category. Thus Saudi Arabia and Indonesia, both predominantly Islamic counties, differ with respect to how modern their views are regarding the status of women. See also Bayly, who forcefully argues that "[f]or development to occur people need to have the belief that they can succeed and that their own societies are essentially benign" (2011: 51).

7 So understood, most of the vociferous critics of "development" raise objections to the *means* by which (and/or through whom) it is brought about, not the *ends* as articulated here. Even when criticizing a focus on economic growth, most such critics are not calling for a return to a preindustrial subsistence economy or premodern health-care practices.

8 In the center of the circle, at low levels of development, rules systems are integrated and informal, overseen by customary leaders; at high levels of development, key aspects become grouped into four largely separate, specialized, and formal domains, crafted and enforced by legal professionals. Similar "separations" occur between state and religious authority, between branches of government, and between science and religion.

9 The enduring power and resonance of Scott (1998) resides in

large part in his documenting of how fully, in the middle decades of the twentieth century, both the political left/right and the global North/South bought into bureaucratic high modernism as the preferred "scheme" for "improving the human condition."

10 Hence Frances Fukuyama could declare the "end of history" in 1989 because, with the collapse of communism as a viable alternative economic system and the triumph of democracy as a political system, history had fulfilled its teleological objectives of converging into the peak forms; all that was left was a bit of (little h) historical tidying up not worthy of a (big H) transformational effort. Needless to say, recent events have not been kind to this thesis.

11 The following paragraphs refine and update passages from Desai and Woolcock (2015). The expression "fragile path of progress" is part of the subtitle of Trebilcock and Daniels (2008).

12 Exemplars of this literature include, among others, Golub (2003), Halliday and Osinsky (2006), Ohnesorge (2007), Haggard et al. (2008), Helmke and Rosenbluth (2009), Armytage (2012), Peerenboom et al. (2012), Hadfield and Weingast (2014), and Marshall (2014).

13 See also Tamanaha (2011: 220), contrasting Peerenboom (2009), for whom the ambiguity at the core of the field is a strength, not a weakness.

14 Respective examples can be found in Raz (1977), Humphreys (2010), and Kratochwil (2014).

15 Situations in which multiple normative or informal legal orders are in place – for example, in disputes over land and water in low-income countries – are often referred to as "legal pluralism"; for an extended discussion of this phenomena and its implications, see Tamanaha (2021a, 2021b).

16 The work of the Building State Capability Program is discussed in more detail in the following chapter.

17 See https://worldjusticeproject.org.

18 See https://namati.org.

19 Staff from these organizations have also contributed to follow-up efforts trying to identify suitable metrics against which countries can benchmark their progress on this goal. Needless to say, finding credible and comparable justice indicators that can be reliably collected and collated by all 193 countries is proving rather difficult. Moreover, policy issues such as crime, where success is measured by its decline, provide powerful incentives for those engaged in policing such activity to under-report

its incidence (since falling rates of crime reflect favorably on their performance). The diligence and dedication of the teams preparing each year's World Justice Report are thus all the more commendable.

20　This section is a revised and extended version of Woolcock (2020).

21　The distinction between technical and non-technical (or "adaptive") problems was made famous by Heifetz (1994); further refinements were outlined in Pritchett and Woolcock (2004) and Andrews et al. (2017).

22　Kauffman's (2016) formally accurate but less elegant formulation is that such solutions are "un-pre-stateable."

23　See Andrews et al. (2017) and Honig (2018) on development efforts generally; on public sector reform specifically see Andrews (2013) and Buntaine et al. (2017).

24　Findings such as these were summarized in World Bank (2015b).

25　An exemplary instance of using mixed methods to assess such an intervention is Rao et al. (2017), who show that while the *average* effect for the intervention was insignificant, there was nonetheless considerable variation around this average (i.e., some groups had significantly improved, others significantly declined), as well as other positive impacts that a single methodological approach alone would not have detected.

26　Or the same machine under the same conditions but in two different time periods, with the second time period characterized by a single change in a single variable.

27　See also the important and detailed arguments laid out in Deaton and Cartwright (2018).

28　More formally, see also Ravallion's (2001) injunction to researchers to "look beyond averages."

29　Assuming five hours of instruction a day, for roughly 200 school days a year, for twelve years.

30　There are well-known methodological problems associated with selecting so-called "positive deviants," but the essence of solid case-study research is selecting appropriately matched comparisons (see Seawright 2016).

31　Such a conclusion circles back to the importance of the process legitimacy concerns raised earlier in this chapter.

32　I return to this issue in the Epilogue, as it pertains to making choices about where and how one might enter the field of development for either professional or volunteering purposes.

33　See Freedman (2015) for a comprehensive analysis of the

strategic "lessons" from war. See also the important new contribution by Blattman (2022).

34 As we noted in Chapter 1, Kleinfeld (2018) makes a very compelling case that sustaining peace in the aftermath of a long-running civil war often entails giving formal power in the new post-war administration to confirmed (former) warlords. One cannot imagine such a "policy implication," no matter how "rigorous" the research on which it is based, ever becoming a formal recommendation of any multilateral institution. The abiding point is that in the most challenging development problems, sound judgment must play a prominent role (Honig 2018).

35 As Hirschman memorably put it, our task is to "treat human beings as something fairly precious and not just something you can play upon. You see, if you ever could figure everything out, if you could have a social science that really is a science, then we would be the first ones to be disappointed. We would be dismayed because if man becomes like that, he could be figured out. And that means that he is not worth as much as we think … Were we ever to succeed, then mankind would have failed!" (cited in Swedberg 1990: 164).

36 For example, the Economic Community of West African States (ECOWAS), the Association of Southeast Asian Nations (ASEAN), the Organization of American States (OAS), et al.

37 Or, more boldly, recognize that development itself is what Hirschman called "a long voyage of discovery"; see the discussion in Woolcock (2019b).

38 See https://successfulsocieties.princeton.edu.

4 Engaging an Increasingly Complex World

1 The rhetorical distinction between "technical" and "adaptive" problems is most famously associated with Heifetz (1994), but, as I discuss below, the spirit of this distinction – and its implications for administration, policy, and practice – have a long history in international development.

2 Useful cases on how to integrate these different types of skills in the quest to enhance the legitimacy and effectiveness of the slum upgrading process can be found in Imparato and Ruster (2003) and Bah et al. (2018). Despite being an omnipresent feature of the development process since the nineteenth century, "slum

upgrading" is, like "building the rule of law," an imperative around which there is a glaring and enduring gap between the prevalence of wide experience and the paucity of actionable knowledge for effectively addressing each new case. It is thus a quintessential example of a complex development challenge: each unhappy case is "unhappy in its own way" (to borrow from Tolstoy) but the imperative to address it cannot be avoided.

3 Parts of this section refine, update, and extend passages from Woolcock (2017). The subtitle comes from Andrews, Pritchett et al. (2014).

4 At no time between 1995 and 2015 did the World Bank have a year when it was *not* engaging in public financial management reforms in Malawi.

5 Most of the projects captured both indicators and related results in a table at the start of the Implementation Completion and Results reports (ICRs). Where indicators and results were not captured in this way, this data was drawn from the results narrative.

6 Indicators were classed as "met" wherever (a) the result as captured in the ICR exceeded or equated to the measure listed in the indicator, or (b) where the summary of results explicitly acknowledged an indicator as achieved. It was necessary to include this later aspect as some of the earlier projects did not consistently capture a quantitatively measurable indicator (e.g., the Institutional Development Project 2 only talks of results, not initial indicators). In these cases, we had to refer to the write up of results to determine whether project implementers considered the result an achievement of what they set out to do or not.

7 See http://www.globalintegrity.org/research/malawi.

8 In 2000, the educational focus of the Millennium Development Goals was on enhancing primary-school enrollment; in 2015, by contrast, the Sustainable Development Goal #4 sought, by 2030, to "ensure inclusive and equitable quality education and promote lifelong learning opportunities for all." If attending school is the first step, the learning objective is vastly more laudable but also correspondingly much more difficult to attain.

9 See Pritchett (2022), updating empirical aspects of Andrews et al. (2017).

10 The passages that follow are adapted from Woolcock and Bridges (2019).

11 See Bridges and Woolcock (2022) for a broader discussion

of the ways in which otherwise laudable imperatives for "measurement," "data," and "evidence" to be the basis of policy nonetheless have limits and weaknesses, most obviously when decisive single numbers – such as the "Doing Business" indicators (used to assess the ease with which firms can be established in any given country), or the scores used to determine eligibility for grants (as opposed to loans) from the World Bank – are subjected to political pressure at levels they cannot bear. Such issues, of course, are not a reason for abandoning measurement, but rather introduce an imperative to "spread risk" by deploying diverse data suites.

12 Namely, the unit homogeneity assumption, which requires those in the "treatment" group to receive identical forms and levels of treatment. This is how drug trials work, for example, but no one in an "adaptive" treatment group, by design, receives "identical" treatment.

13 In the terminology used in earlier chapters, it can be said that CDD projects are efforts by "big development" to use "small development" means to attain "national development" ends.

14 See Antlöv et al. (2016). Guggenheim (2021) provides a fuller accounting of the origin and evolution of attempts by the World Bank to operationalize social development issues upon hiring its first sociologist, Michael Cernea, in 1974. The largest, most prominent, and enduring instantiation of operationalized social theory at the World Bank (and elsewhere) is "community-driven development." Guggenheim was the primary architect of the KDP.

15 See also Gibson and Woolcock (2008), who provide a more detailed mechanisms-based account of how the KDP's deliberative processes functioned.

16 See Brixi et al. (2015), who explicitly use this approach to map and explain subnational variation in the quality of service delivery across the otherwise highly centralized countries of the Middle East and North Africa.

17 To be sure, certain technical solutions to technical problems (e.g., macroeconomic reforms, road-building procedures) are likely to transfer across borders, and in the most desperate of circumstances (e.g., refugee camps and peacekeeping missions in fragile states) the ethical imperative to act now may override concerns about how to build implementation capability in the long run. Even so, the important work of Campbell (2018) on operational dynamics in these most testing of circumstances

finds that the most effective field offices are those that are given maximum discretion to respond to contextual idiosyncrasies. See also the impressive list of case studies on unlikely implementation successes prepared by Innovations for Successful Societies, overseen by Jennifer Widner at Princeton University (https://successfulsocieties.princeton.edu).

18 Aspects of this section revise and extend passages from Woolcock (2019b)

19 See also Hirschman and Lindblom (1962).

20 Kauffman (2016: 2) defines such problems as "unprestatable" (which is equally inelegant, but accurate nonetheless), referring to challenges so complex that no manner of experience, evidence, intelligence, preparation, or wisdom could have anticipated the problems associated with trying to solve them. The more popular expression is that deeply complex challenges are replete with unknown unknowns.

21 That is, social science aping (a version of) the physical sciences, in which the world is viewed as a "machine" whose underlying causal mechanisms are optimally apprehended by isolating and analyzing its constituent "parts."

22 See Hodge (2007), Mitchell (2002), and Easterly (2014).

23 The full scholarly foundations and operational procedures of PDIA are provided in Andrews at el. (2017); further details on the countries and sectors in which PDIA has been applied can be found on the website of the Building State Capability program, based in the Center for International Development at Harvard University (https://bsc.cid.harvard.edu). In keeping with earlier arguments, it is clear that PDIA *can* work; it regards itself as a perpetual "second word" (not a deeply original "first word," or a decisively proven "final word") on how to enhance state capability for policy implementation.

24 A summary of this assessment is available at https://blog-pfm .imf.org/pfmblog/2022/01/-pfm-reform-through-pdia-what -works-and-when-it-works-.html.

25 According to Google Scholar citation counts, as processed by Harzing's "Publish or Perish" software program. The most cited is, appropriately enough for this book, Joseph Schumpeter's (1934) *The Theory of Economic Development*, which emphasizes both the "creative" and the "destructive" nature of the development process.

26 On this point, and its associated consequences, see Rao and Woolcock (2007).

27 Details on the Concert of Europe's history, structure, operating procedures, and effectiveness can be found in Elrod (1976) and Mazower (2013). See also Talbott (2009).

28 See Reynolds (2009: Chapter 3) on the events of 1944, and especially the summit at Yalta, that shaped these negotiations. For an insightful interpretation of events and negotiations that preceded by several years the formation of the IMF and World Bank at Bretton Woods in July 1944, see Helleiner (2014). See also Steil (2013).

Epilogue

1 From an interview originally published in the *Harvard Gazette*, May 18, 2018, but republished shortly after Farmer's untimely death in February 2022.

2 Formally, many such higher-order claims are deontological, meaning that they reflect normative obligations or duties, grounded in adherence to ethical rules, not the consequences of action. Classic examples include the International Declaration of Human Rights and the biblical Ten Commandments: we broadly uphold the importance of honoring our parents not because "rigorous empirical evidence" suggests it is (or is not!) prudent to do so, but because we believe it is normatively right and proper.

3 From time to time, one hears of "experiments" in which a group of devout "believers" is randomly assigned to one of two hospitals with patients suffering from similar afflictions, and asked to pray for those patients... You get the idea. Such cases are instructive only to the extent they are graphic instances of the veracity of a higher-order knowledge claim being erroneously subjected to the epistemological logics of lower-order claims.

4 The importance of learning to "give *and* receive" – generally, but in development work in particular – is stressed in the opening chapter of Klitgaard (1990).

5 As noted earlier, see Kleinfeld (2018) and Blattman (2022) on how endemic violence ends.

6 In Woolcock (2007), I argued that the three key skills and sensibilities that graduate students in development need to be taught (and acquire) are those of the "detective" (problem-solver), the "translator" (communicator between different groups making

different kinds of knowledge claims), and the "diplomat" (doing deals, resolving disputes between those with seemingly different understandings of how the world works). Here I lay out a more formal analytical distinction between these categories, which correspond, respectively, to filling space, connecting space, and protecting space.

7 One interpretation of the British movie *I, Daniel Blake* (2016) is that it powerfully conveys how enduring and pervasive complex implementation issues are in rich countries, let alone poor ones.

References

Acemoglu, Daron and James Robinson (2019) *The Narrow Corridor: States, Societies, and the Fate of Liberty*, New York: Penguin.

Acemoglu, Daron, Simon Johnson, and James Robinson (2001) "The colonial origins of comparative development: an empirical investigation," *American Economic Review* 91(5): 1369–401.

Adichie, Chimamanda Ngozi (2009) "The danger of a single story," TED talk, at https://www.ted.com/talks /chimamanda_ngozi_adichie_the_danger_of_a_single_story ?language=en.

Adler, Daniel, Caroline Sage, and Michael Woolcock (2009) "Interim institutions and the development process: opening spaces for reform in Cambodia and Indonesia," University of Manchester: Brooks World Poverty Institute Working Paper 86.

Aghion, Philippe and Alexandra Roulet (2014) "Growth and the smart state," *Annual Review of Economics* 6: 913–92.

Aghion, Philippe, Celine Antonin, and Simon Bunel (2020) *The Power of Creative Destruction: Economic Upheaval and the Wealth of Nations*, Cambridge, MA: Harvard University Press.

Alesina, Alberto and Edward Glaeser (2004) *Fighting Poverty in the US and Europe: A World of Difference*, New York: Oxford University Press.

Allen, Robert C. (2009) "Engels' pause: technical change,

capital accumulation, and inequality in the British industrial revolution," *Explorations in Economic History* 46(4):
418–35.

Andrews, Matt (2013) *The Limits of Institutional Reform
in Development: Changing Rules for Realistic Solutions*,
New York: Cambridge University Press.

Andrews, Matt, Lant Pritchett, and Michael Woolcock (2017)
Building State Capability: Evidence, Analysis, Action,
New York: Oxford University Press.

Andrews, Matt, Lant Pritchett, Salimah Samji, and Michael
Woolcock (2014) "Capability traps in development: how
initiatives to improve administrative systems succeed at
failing," *Prism* 3(3): 63–74.

Andrews, Matt, Marco Cangiano, Neil Cole, Paulo De
Renzio, Philip Krause, and Renaud Seligmann (2014) "This
is PFM," Harvard University: CID Working Paper No. 285.

Ang, Yuen Yuen (2016) *How China Escaped the Poverty
Trap*, Ithaca, NY: Cornell University Press.

Antlöv, Hans, Anna Wetterberg, and Leni Dharmawan (2016)
"Village governance, community life, and the 2014 Village
Law in Indonesia," *Bulletin of Indonesian Economic
Studies* 52(2): 161–83.

Appleby, Joyce (2010) *The Relentless Revolution: A History
of Capitalism*, New York: W. W. Norton.

April, Leah, Caroline Hughes, Nicola Smithers, Sokbunthoeun
So, and Michael Woolcock (eds.) (2018) *Alternative
Paths to Public Financial Management and Public Sector
Reform: Experiences from East Asia*, Washington, DC:
World Bank.

Ariadharma, Erwin and Hari Purnomo (2018) "Indonesia:
leveraging best practices and experimentation in Public
Financial Management and Public Sector Reforms in
post-Asian financial crisis context," in Leah April et al.
(eds.) *Alternative Paths to Public Financial Management
and Public Sector Reform: Experiences from East Asia*,
Washington, DC: World Bank, pp. 41–57.

Armitage, David (2012) *Foundations of Modern International
Thought*, New York: Cambridge University Press.

Armytage, Livingston (2012) *Reforming Justice: A Journey*

to Fairness in Asia, New York: Cambridge University Press.

Bah, El-hadj M., Issa Faye, and Zekebweliwai F. Geh (eds.) (2018) *Housing Market Dynamics in Africa*, London: Palgrave Macmillan.

Bain, Katherine, David Booth, and Leni Wild (2016) "Doing development differently at the World Bank: updating the plumbing to fit the architecture," London: Overseas Development Institute.

Banerjee, Abhijit and Lakshmi Iyer (2005) "History, institutions, and economic performance: the legacy of colonial land tenure systems in India," *American Economic Review* 95(4): 1190–213.

Barma, Naazneen H., Elisabeth Huybens, and Lorena Viñuela (eds.) (2014) *Institutions Taking Root: Building State Capacity in Challenging Contexts*, Washington, DC: World Bank.

Barron, Patrick, Claire Q. Smith, and Michael Woolcock (2004) "Understanding local level conflict in developing countries: theory, evidence and implications from Indonesia," World Bank: Social Development Papers, Conflict Prevention and Reconstruction, No. 19.

Barron, Patrick, Rachael Diprose, and Michael Woolcock (2011) *Contesting Development: Participatory Projects and Local Conflict Dynamics in Indonesia*, New Haven: Yale University Press.

Barth, James R., Gerard Caprio Jr, and Ross Levine (2012) *Guardians of Finance: Making Regulators Work for Us*, Cambridge, MA: MIT Press.

Bates, Robert (1981) *Markets and States in Tropical Africa: The Political Basis of Agricultural Policies*, Berkeley: University of California Press.

Bates, Robert (2010) *Violence and Prosperity: A Political Economy of Development*, 2nd ed., New York: W. W. Norton.

Bates, Robert H. (2021) *The Political Economy of Development: A Game Theoretic Approach*, New York: Cambridge University Press.

Bayly, C. A. (2004) *The Birth of the Modern World*

1780–1914: Global Connections and Comparisons, Oxford: Blackwell.

Bayly, C. A. (2011) "Indigenous and colonial origins of comparative economic development: the case of colonial India and Africa," in C. A. Bayly, Simon Szreter, Vijayendra Rao, and Michael Woolcock (eds.) *History, Historians and Development Policy: A Necessary Dialogue,* Manchester: Manchester University Press, pp. 39–64.

Bayly, C. A. (2018) *Remaking the Modern World 1900–2015: Global Connections and Comparisons,* Malden, MA: Wiley Blackwell.

Behn, Robert D. (2017) "How scientific is 'the science of delivery'?" *Canadian Public Administration* 60(1): 89–110.

Benton, Lauren (2002) *Law and Colonial Cultures,* New York: Cambridge University Press.

Berger, John (1972) *Ways of Seeing,* London: Penguin.

Berry, Marie E. (2015) "When 'bright futures' fade: paradoxes of women's empowerment in Rwanda," *Signs: Journal of Women in Culture and Society* 41(1): 1–27.

Bertlesmann Transformation Index (BTI) (2020a) This and subsequent annual reports are available at https://bti-project .org/en.

Bertlesmann Transformation Index (BTI) (2020b) "Resistance to democratic regression and authoritarian rule is growing," at https://bti-project.org/content/en/reports/global-report -d/global_findings_democracy_2020_EN.pdf.

Besley, Timothy (2020) "State capacity, reciprocity and the social contract," LSE Working Paper.

Besley, Timothy and Torsten Persson (2009) "The origins of state capacity: property rights, taxation and politics," *American Economic Review* 99(4): 1218–44.

Bingham, Tom (2010) *The Rule of Law,* London: Allen Lane.

Blattman, Christopher (2022) *Why We Fight: The Roots of War and the Paths to Peace,* New York: Viking.

Bolt, Jutta and Jan Luiten Van Zanden (2020) "Maddison style estimates of the evolution of the world economy: a new 2020 update," Maddison Project Working Paper WP-15.

Bridges, Kate and Michael Woolcock (2017) "How (not) to fix problems that matter: assessing and responding to Malawi's history of institutional reform," Policy Research Working Paper No. 8289, Washington, DC: World Bank.

Bridges, Kate and Michael Woolcock (2019) "Implementing adaptive approaches in real world scenarios: a Nigeria case study, with lessons for theory and practice," Policy Research Working Paper No. 8904, Washington, DC: World Bank.

Bridges, Kate and Michael Woolcock (2022) "Measuring what matters: principles for a balanced data suite that prioritizes problem-solving and learning," Policy Research Working Paper No. 10051, Washington, DC: World Bank.

Brinkerhoff, Derick W. and Marcus D. Ingle (1989) "Integrating blueprint and process: a structured flexibility approach to development management," *Public Administration and Development* 9(5): 487–503.

Brixi, Hana, Ellen Lust, and Michael Woolcock (2015) *Trust, Voice and Incentives: Learning from Local Success Stories in Public Service Delivery in the Middle East and North Africa*, Washington, DC: World Bank.

Buchanan, Allen and Robert O. Keohane (2006) "The legitimacy of global governance institutions," *Ethics & International Affairs* 20(4): 405–37.

Buntaine, Mark T., Bradley C. Parks, and Benjamin P. Buch (2017) "Aiming at the wrong targets: the domestic consequences of international efforts to build institutions," *International Studies Quarterly* 61(2): 471–88.

Burrow, John (2008) *A History of Histories*, New York: Vintage.

Bussolo, Maurizio, Maria Eugenia Dávalos, Vito Peragine, and Ramya Sundaram (2019) *Toward a New Social Contract: Taking on Distributional Tensions in Europe and Central Asia*, Washington, DC: World Bank.

Cameron, Elizabeth E., Jennifer B. Nuzzo, and Jessica A. Bell (2019) *Global Health Security Index: Building Collective Action and Accountability*, Baltimore, MD: Johns Hopkins, Bloomberg School of Public Health.

Campbell, Susanna (2018) *Global Governance and Local*

Peace: Accountability and Performance in International Peacekeeping, New York: Cambridge University Press.

Carothers, Tom (ed.) (2006) *Promoting the Rule of Law Abroad: In Search of Knowledge*, Washington, DC: Carnegie Endow. Int. Peace.

Cartwright, Nancy (2007) "Are RCTs the gold standard?" *BioSocieties* 2(1): 11–20.

Case, Anne and Angus Deaton (2020) *Deaths of Despair and the Future of Capitalism*, Princeton, NJ: Princeton University Press.

Casey, Katherine (2018) "Radical decentralization: does community-driven development work?" *Annual Review of Economics* 10: 139–63.

Casey, Katherine, Rachel Glennerster, and Edward Miguel (2012) "Reshaping institutions: evidence on aid impacts using a pre-analysis plan," *The Quarterly Journal of Economics* 127(4): 1755–812.

Catão, Luís A. and Maurice Obstfeld (eds.) (2019) *Meeting Globalization's Challenges: Policies to Make Trade Work for All*, Princeton, NJ: Princeton University Press.

Chandy, Laurence, Hiroshi Kato, and Homi Kharas (eds.) (2015) *The Last Mile in Ending Extreme Poverty*, Washington, DC: Brookings Institution Press.

Clarke, Daniel J. and Stefan Dercon (2016) *Dull Disasters: How Planning Ahead Will Make a Difference*, New York: Oxford University Press.

Cohen, Michael and Robert W. Shenton (1996) *Doctrines of Development*, London: Routledge.

Comaroff, John L. and Jean Comaroff (2004) "Criminal justice, cultural justice: the limits of liberalism and the pragmatics of difference in the new South Africa," *American Ethnologist* 31(2): 188–204.

Cooper, Hilary and Simon Szreter (2021) *After the Virus: Lessons from the Past for a Better Future*, Cambridge: Cambridge University Press.

Copestake, James, Marlies Morsink, and Fiona Remnant (eds.) (2019) *Attributing Development Impact: The Qualitative Impact Protocol (QuIP) Case Book*, Rugby: Practical Action Publishing.

Corral, David, Alexander Irwin, Nandini Krishnan, Daniel Gerszon Mahler, and Tara Vishwanath (2020) *Fragility and Violence: On the Front Lines of the Fight Against Poverty*, Washington, DC: World Bank.

Cronon, William (1983) *Changes in the Land: Indians, Colonists, and the Ecology of New England*, New York: Hill and Wang.

Daedalus (1998) Special issue on "Early modernities," *Daedalus* 127(3).

Daedalus (2000) Special issue on "Multiple modernities," *Daedalus* 129(1).

Davis, Wade (2009) *The Wayfinders: Why Ancient Wisdom Matters in the Modern World*, Toronto: House of Anansi Press.

De Soto, Hernando (2000) *The Mystery of Capital: Why Capitalism Triumphs in the West and Fails Everywhere Else*, New York: Civitas Books.

De Vries, Jan (2008) *The Industrious Revolution*, New York: Cambridge University Press.

De Waal, Alex (2015) *The Real Politics of Africa: Money, War and the Business of Power*, Cambridge: Polity Press.

Deaton, Angus and Nancy Cartwright (2018) "Understanding and misunderstanding randomized controlled trials," *Social Science & Medicine* 210: 2–21.

Dell, Melissa (2010) "The persistent effects of Peru's mining mita," *Econometrica* 78(6): 1863–903.

Dell, Melissa, Nathan Lane, and Pablo Querubin (2018) "The historical state, local collective action, and economic development in Vietnam," *Econometrica* 86(6): 2083–121.

Desai, Deval (2014) "In search of 'hire' knowledge: hiring practices and the organization of knowledge in a rule of law field," in David Marshall (ed.) *The International Rule of Law Movement: A Crisis of Legitimacy and the Way Forward*, Cambridge, MA: Harvard Law School (Human Rights Program Series), pp. 42–83.

Desai, Deval and Michael Woolcock (2015) "Experimental justice reform: lessons from the World Bank and beyond," *Annual Review of Law and Social Science* 11: 155–74.

Dirks, Nicholas B. (2001) *Castes of Mind: Colonialism and*

the Making of Modern India, Princeton, NJ: Princeton University Press.

Drèze, Jean and Amartya Sen (1995) India: Economic Development and Social Opportunity, Delhi: Oxford University Press.

Easterly, William (2014) The Tyranny of Experts: Economists, Dictators, and the Forgotten Rights of the Poor, New York: Basic Books.

Eliot, T. S. (1943) "Little Gidding" in Four Quartets, San Diego: Harcourt.

Elrod, Richard B. (1976) "The concert of Europe: a fresh look at an international system," World Politics 28(2): 159–74.

Escobar, Arturo (1995) Encountering Development: The Making and Unmaking of the Third World, Princeton, NJ: Princeton University Press.

Eyal, Gil (2019) The Crisis of Expertise, Cambridge: Polity Press.

Ferguson, James (1990) The Anti-Politics Machine: Development, Depoliticization, and Bureaucratic Power in Lesotho, New York: Cambridge University Press.

Flyvbjerg, Bent and Cass Sunstein (2015) "The principle of the malevolent hiding hand; or, the planning fallacy writ large," Social Research: An International Quarterly 83(4): 979–1004.

Fox, Jonathan (2020) "Contested terrain: international development projects and countervailing power for the excluded," World Development 133.

Freedman, Lawrence (2015) Strategy: A History, Oxford: Oxford University Press.

Freedom House (2020) Freedom in the World. An annual report, at https://bti-project.org/en.

Frieden, Jeffry (2020) Global Capitalism: Its Fall and Rise in the Twentieth Century, and its Stumbles in the Twenty-First, New York: W. W. Norton & Company.

Fukuyama, Francis (1995) Trust: The Social Virtues and the Creation of Prosperity, New York: The Free Press.

Fukuyama, Francis (2011) The Origins of Political Order: From Prehuman Times to the French Revolution, New York: Farrar, Straus and Giroux.

Fukuyama, Francis (2014) *Political Order and Political Decay: From the Industrial Revolution to the Globalization of Democracy*, New York: Farrar, Straus and Giroux.

Galor, Oded (2022) *The Journey of Humanity: The Origins of Wealth and Inequality*, New York: Dutton.

Gauri, Varun, Michael Woolcock, and Deval Desai (2013) "Intersubjective meaning and collective action in developing societies: theory, evidence and policy implications," *Journal of Development Studies* 49(1): 160–72.

Gawande, Atul (2017) "The heroism of incremental care," *The New Yorker*, January 15, at https://www.newyorker.com/magazine/2017/01/23/the-heroism-of-incremental-care.

Geithner, Timothy (2014) *Stress Test: Reflections on Financial Crises*, New York: Crown Publishers.

Gibson, Christopher and Michael Woolcock (2008) "Empowerment, deliberative development and local level politics in Indonesia: participatory projects as a source of countervailing power," *Studies in Comparative International Development* 43(2): 151–80.

Giridharadas, Anand (2019) *Winners Take All: The Elite Charade of Changing the World*, New York: Vintage.

Golub, Stephen (2003) "Beyond rule of law orthodoxy: the legal empowerment alternative," Carnegie Endowment for International Peace, Rule of Law Series Working Papers Number 41, October.

Graeber, David and David Wengrow (2021) *The Dawn of Everything: A New History of Humanity*, London: Penguin.

Groopman, Jerome (2007) *How Doctors Think*, Boston: Houghton Mifflin Harcourt.

Guggenheim, Scott (2006) "Crises and contradictions: understanding the origins of a community development project in Indonesia," in Anthony Bebbington et al. (eds.) *The Search for Empowerment: Social Capital as Idea and Practice at the World Bank*, Bloomfield, CT: Kumarian Press, pp. 111–44.

Guggenheim, Scott (2021) "Putting people first in practice: Indonesia and the Kecamatan Development Program," in Marita Koch-Weser and Scott Guggenheim (eds.) *Social*

Development in the World Bank: Essays in Honor of Michael M. Cernea, London: Springer Nature, pp. 177–89.

Hadfield, Gillian and Barry Weingast (2014) "Microfoundations of the rule of law," *Annual Review of Political Science* 17: 21–42.

Haggard, Stephan, Andrew MacIntyre, and Lydia Tiede (2008) "The rule of law and economic development," *Annual Review of Political Science* 11: 205–34.

Hagmann, Tobias and Markus V. Hoehne (2009) "Failures of the state failure debate: evidence from the Somali territories," *Journal of International Development* 21(1): 42–57.

Halliday, Terence C. and Pavel Osinsky (2006) "Globalization of law," *Annual Review of Sociology* 32: 447–70.

Hallward-Driemeier, Mary and Lant Pritchett (2015) "How business is done in the developing world: deals versus rules," *Journal of Economic Perspectives* 29(3): 121–40.

Harper, Timothy (2011) "The tools of transition: education and development in modern Southeast Asian history," in C. A. Bayly, Vijayendra Rao, Simon Szreter, and Michael Woolcock (eds.) *History, Historians and Development Policy: A Necessary Dialogue*, Manchester: University of Manchester Press, pp. 193–212.

Harrison, Peter (1999) "'Subduing the earth': Genesis 1, early modern science, and the exploitation of nature," *The Journal of Religion* 79(1): 86–109.

Hart, Gillian (2001) "Development critiques in the 1990s: culs de sac and promising paths," *Progress in Human Geography* 25(4): 649–58.

Hathaway, Oona A. and Scott J. Shapiro (2017) *The Internationalists: How a Radical Plan to Outlaw War Remade the World*, New York: Simon and Schuster.

Hausmann, Ricardo, Carlo Pietrobelli, and Miguel Angel Santos (2021) "Place-specific determinants of income gaps: new sub-national evidence from Mexico," *Journal of Business Research* 131: 782–92.

Heifetz, Ronald (1994) *Leadership Without Easy Answers*, Cambridge, MA: Harvard University Press.

Helleiner, Eric (2014) *Forgotten Foundations of Bretton*

Woods: International Development and the Making of the Postwar Order, Ithaca, NY: Cornell University Press.

Heller, Patrick (2020) "A virus, social democracy, and dividends for Kerala," *The Hindu*, April 18, at https://www.thehindu.com/opinion/lead/a-virus-social-democracy-and-dividends-for-kerala/article31370554.ece.

Helmke, Gretchen and Frances Rosenbluth (2009) "Regimes and the rule of law: judicial independence in comparative perspective," *Annual Review of Political Science* 12: 345–66.

Heryanto, Ariel (1988) "The development of development," *Indonesia* 46: 1–27.

Hessler, Peter (2022) "China's reform generation adapts to life in the middle class," *The New Yorker*, January 3 and 10.

Hickey, Sam (2011) "The politics of social protection: what do we get from a 'social contract' approach?" *Canadian Journal of Development Studies* 32(4): 426–38.

Hindle, Steve (2004) *On the Parish? The Micro-Politics of Poor Relief in Rural England c. 1550–1750*, Oxford: Oxford University Press.

Hirschman, Albert O. (1958) *The Strategy of Economic Development*, New Haven: Yale University Press.

Hirschman, Albert O. (1968) *Development Projects Observed*, Washington, DC: Brookings Institution Press.

Hirschman, Albert O. (1995) Preface to *Development Projects Observed*, Washington, DC: Brookings Institution Press.

Hirschman, Albert O. and Charles Lindblom (1962) "Economic development, research and development, policy making: some converging views," *Behavioral Science* 7(2): 211–12.

Hodge, Joseph Morgan (2007) *Triumph of the Expert: Agrarian Doctrines of Development and the Legacies of British Colonialism*, Athens: Ohio University Press.

Honig, Dan (2018) *Navigation by Judgment: Why and When Top-Down Management of Foreign Aid Doesn't Work*, New York: Oxford University Press.

Honig, Dan (forthcoming) *Mission Driven Bureaucrats*, New York: Oxford University Press.

Hughes, Austin L. (2012) "The folly of scientism," *The New Atlantis: A Journal of Technology and Society* 37: 32–50.

Humphreys, Stephen (2010) *Theatre of the Rule of Law: Transnational Legal Intervention in Theory and Practice*, Cambridge: Cambridge University Press.

Huntington, Samuel (1968) *Political Order in Changing Societies*, New Haven: Yale University Press.

Imparato, Ivo and Jeff Ruster (2003) *Slum Upgrading and Participation: Lessons from Latin America*, Washington, DC: World Bank.

Isser, Deborah (2011) "Understanding and engaging customary justice systems," in Deborah Isser (ed.) *Customary Justice and the Rule of Law in War-Torn Societies*, Washington, DC: US Institute for Peace, pp. 325–67.

Jackson, Matthew O. (2019) *The Human Network: How Your Social Position Determines Your Power, Beliefs, and Behaviors*, New York: Pantheon Books.

Kagan, Robert (2018) *The Jungle Grows Back: America and Our Imperiled World*, New York: Alfred A. Knopf.

Kahneman, Daniel (2011) *Thinking, Fast and Slow*, London: Macmillan.

Kaneko, Yuka, Narufumi Kadomatsu, and Brian Tamanaha (eds.) (2022) *Land Law and Disputes in Asia: In Search of an Alternative for Development*, New York: Routledge.

Kapur, Devesh, Chandra Bhan Prasad, Lant Pritchett, and D. Shyam Babu (2010) "Rethinking inequality: Dalits in Uttar Pradesh in the market reform era," *Economic and Political Weekly* 45(35): 39–49.

Katz, Michael B. (2013) *The Undeserving Poor: America's Enduring Confrontation with Poverty*, 2nd ed., New York: Oxford University Press.

Kauffman, Stuart (2016) *Humanity in a Creative Universe*, New York: Oxford University Press.

Khālidī, Tarīf (1981) "The idea of progress in classical Islam," *Journal of Near Eastern Studies* 40(4): 277–89.

Khan, Mushtaq (2018) "Political settlements and the analysis of institutions," *African Affairs* 117(469): 636–55.

Kleinfeld, Rachel (2018) *A Savage Order: How the World's*

Deadliest Countries Can Forge a Path to Security, New York: Pantheon Books.

Klitgaard, Robert (1990) *Tropical Gangsters: One Man's Experience with Development and Decadence in Deepest Africa*, New York: Basic Books.

Krastev, Ivan and Stephen Holmes (2019) *The Light That Failed: Why the West is Losing the Fight for Democracy*, New York: Pegasus Books.

Kratochwil, Friedrich (2014) *The Status of Law in World Society: Meditations on the Role and Rule of Law*, Cambridge: Cambridge University Press.

Krishna, Anirudh (2011) *One Illness Away: Why People Become Poor and How They Escape Poverty*, New York: Oxford University Press.

Kristof, Nicholas D. and Sheryl WuDunn (2020) *Tightrope: Americans Reaching for Hope*, New York: Knopf.

Krugman, Paul (1994) "The fall and rise of development economics," in Lloyd Rodwin and Donald Schon (eds.) *Rethinking the Development Experience: Essays Provoked by the Work of Albert O. Hirschman*, Washington, DC: Brookings Institution Press, pp. 39–58.

Krygier, Martin (2012) "Why the Rule of Law is too important to be left to lawyers," *Prawo i Więź* 2: 30–52.

Krygier, Martin (2015) "Rule of law and Rechtsstaat," in J. D. Wright (ed.) *Encyclopedia of the Social and Behavioral Sciences*, 2nd ed., Atlanta, GA: Elsevier.

Kuznets, Simon (1966) *Modern Economic Growth: Rate, Structure, and Spread*, New Haven: Yale University Press.

La Porta, Rafael, Florencio Lopez-de-Silanes, and Andrei Shleifer (2008) "The economic consequences of legal origins," *Journal of Economic Literature* 46(2): 285–332.

Larkins, Erika Robb (2015) *The Spectacular Favela: Violence in Modern Brazil*, Berkeley: University of California Press.

Lasch, Christopher (1991) *The True and Only Heaven: Progress and its Critics*, New York: W. W. Norton & Co.

Lee, Alexander (2019) "Land, state capacity and colonialism: evidence from India," *Comparative Political Studies* 52(3): 412–44.

Lees, Lynn Hollen (1998) *The Solidarities of Strangers: The*

English Poor Laws and the People, 1700–1948, New York: Cambridge University Press.

Leonard, Dorothy and Sylvia Sensiper (1998) "The role of tacit knowledge in group innovation," *California Management Review* 40(3): 112–32.

Levi, Margaret (2018) "The who, what, and why of performance-based legitimacy," *Journal of Intervention and Statebuilding* 12(4): 603–10.

Levi, Margaret, Audrey Sacks, and Tom Tyler (2009) "Conceptualizing legitimacy, measuring legitimating beliefs," *American Behavioral Scientist* 53(3): 354–75.

Levitsky, Steven and Daniel Ziblatt (2018) *How Democracies Die*, New York: Penguin Random House.

Lewis, David (2019) "'Big D' and 'little d': two types of twenty-first century development?" *Third World Quarterly* 40(11): 1957–75.

Lindblom, Charles (1959) "The science of muddling through," *Public Administration Review* 19(2): 79–88.

Lindblom, Charles (1979) "Still muddling, not yet through," *Public Administration Review* 39(6): 517–26.

Lowes, Sara and Eduardo Montero (2017) "Mistrust in medicine: the legacy of colonial medicine campaigns in Central Africa," Working paper, Bocconi University.

Macaulay, Stewart (1963) "Non-contractual relations in business: a preliminary study," *American Sociological Review* 28(1): 55–67.

McDonnell, Erin Metz (2020) *Patchwork Leviathan: Pockets of Bureaucratic Effectiveness in Developing States*, Princeton, NJ: Princeton University Press.

McGovern, Mike (2012) *Unmasking the State: Making Guinea Modern*, Chicago: University of Chicago Press.

McGregor, Douglas (1960) *The Human Side of Enterprise*, New York: McGraw-Hill.

Mansuri, Ghazala and Vijayendra Rao (2012) *Localizing Development*, Washington, DC: World Bank.

Marshall, David (ed.) (2014) *The International Rule of Law Movement: A Crisis of Legitimacy and the Way Forward*, Cambridge, MA: Harvard Law School (Human Rights Program Series).

Matin, Imran (2022) "What 'cash-plus' programs teach us about fighting extreme poverty," *Stanford Social Innovation Review*, January 5.

Mattes, Robert (2020) "Lived poverty on the rise: decade of living-standard gains ends in Africa," Afrobarometer Policy Paper No. 62.

Mazower, Mark (2013) *Governing the World: The History of an Idea, 1815 to the Present*, New York: Penguin.

Menkhaus, Ken (2007) "Governance without government in Somalia: spoilers, state building, and the politics of coping," *International Security* 31(3): 74–106.

Merry, Sally Engle (1988) "Legal pluralism," *Law & Society Review* 22(5): 869–96.

Migdal, Joel (1988) *Strong States and Weak Societies: State-Society Relations and State Capabilities in the Third World*, Princeton, NJ: Princeton University Press.

Migdal, Joel (2001) *State in Society: Studying How States and Societies Transform and Constitute One Another*, New York: Cambridge University Press.

Mitchell, Timothy (2002) *Rule of Experts: Egypt, Techno-Politics, Modernity*, Berkeley: University of California Press.

Moore, Barrington (1965) *The Social Origins of Dictatorship and Democracy*, Boston: Beacon Press.

Moran, Mark (2016) *Serious Whitefella Stuff: When Solutions Became the Problem in Indigenous Affairs*, Melbourne: Melbourne University Press.

Mueller, Hannes and Chanon Techasunthornwat (2020) "Conflict and poverty," Background paper for Poverty and Shared Prosperity Report 2020, Washington DC: World Bank.

Newell, Sasha (2012) *The Modernity Bluff: Crime, Consumption, and Citizenship in Cote d'Ivoire*, Chicago: University of Chicago Press.

Nichols, Tom (2018) *The Death of Expertise: The Campaign against Established Knowledge and Why it Matters*, New York: Oxford University Press.

Nisbet, Robert (1980) *History of the Idea of Progress*, New York: Basic Books.

North, Douglass C., John J. Wallis, and Barry R. Weingast

(2009) *Violence and Social Orders: A Conceptual Framework for Interpreting Recorded Human History*, New York: Cambridge University Press.

Nunn, Nathan (2008) "The long-term effects of Africa's slave trades," *Quarterly Journal of Economics* 123(1): 139–76.

Nunn, Nathan (2020) "The historical roots of economic development," *Science* 367: 1441–48.

Nunn, Nathan and Leonard Wantchekon (2011) "The slave trade and the origins of mistrust in Africa," *American Economic Review* 101(7): 3221–52.

O'Toole, Fintan (2021) "The lie of nation building," *New York Review of Books*, October 7.

Ohnesorge, John (2007) "The rule of law," *Annual Review of Law and Social Science* 3: 99–114.

Palmer, Ada (2017) "On progress and historical change," *Know: A Journal on the Formation of Knowledge* 1(2): 319–37.

Peerenboom, Randall (2009) "The future of rule of law: challenges and prospects for the field," *Hague Journal of the Rule of Law* 1(1): 5–14.

Peerenboom, Randall, Michael Zürn, and André Nollkaemper (2012) "Conclusion: from rule of law promotion to rule of law dynamics," in Michael Zürn, André Nollkaemper, and Randall Peerenboom (eds.) *Rule of Law Dynamics in an Era of International and Transnational Governance*, Cambridge: Cambridge University Press, pp. 305–24.

Petrova, Bilyana (2020) "Redistribution and the quality of government: evidence from Central and Eastern Europe," *British Journal of Political Science* 51(1): 374–93.

Philippon, Thomas (2019) *The Great Reversal: How America Gave Up on Free Markets*, Cambridge, MA: Harvard University Press.

Pincus, Steve (2009) *1688: The First Modern Revolution*, New Haven: Yale University Press.

Pirie, Fernanda (2021) *The Rule of Laws: A 4,000-Year Quest to Order the World*, New York: Basic Books.

Pistor, Katarina (2019) *The Code of Capital: How Law Creates Wealth and Inequality*, Princeton, NJ: Princeton University Press.

Pitts, Jennifer (2005) *A Turn to Empire: The Rise of Imperial Liberalism in Britain and France*, Princeton, NJ: Princeton University Press.

Polanyi, Karl (1944) *The Great Transformation*, Boston: Beacon Press.

Polanyi, Michael (1966) *The Tacit Dimension*, Chicago: University of Chicago Press.

Pomeranz, Kenneth (2001) *The Great Divergence: China, Europe, and the Making of the Modern World Economy*, Princeton, NJ: Princeton University Press.

Pritchett, Lant (1997) "Divergence, big time," *Journal of Economic Perspectives* 11(3): 3–17.

Pritchett, Lant (2014) "The risks to education systems from design mismatch and global isomorphism: concepts, with examples from India," WIDER Working Paper No. 2014/039, Helsinki: UNU-WIDER.

Pritchett, Lant (2020a) "Trends in state capability, 1996–2018: an update of national indicators," Background paper prepared for the Poverty and Shared Prosperity Report 2020, Washington, DC: World Bank.

Pritchett, Lant (2020b) "The big stuck, updated," Building State Capability Program, Harvard Kennedy School, Blog post, June 3, at https://buildingstatecapability.com/2020/06/03/the-big-stuck-updated.

Pritchett, Lant (2020c) "Randomizing development: method or madness?," in Florent Bédécarrats, Isabelle Guérin, and François Roubard (eds.) *Randomized Control Trials in the Field of Development: Critical Perspectives*, Oxford: Oxford University Press, pp. 79–107.

Pritchett, Lant (2022) "National development delivers: And how! And how?" *Economic Modelling* 107: 105717.

Pritchett, Lant and Michael Woolcock (2004) "Solutions when the solution is the problem: arraying the disarray in development," *World Development* 32(2): 191–212.

Pritchett, Lant, Kunal Sen, and Eric Werker (eds.) (2018) *Deals and Development: The Political Dynamics of Growth Episodes*, New York: Oxford University Press.

Pritchett, Lant, Michael Woolcock, and Matt Andrews (2013) "Looking like a state: techniques of persistent failure in state capability for implementation," *Journal of Development Studies* 49(1): 1–18.

Przeworski, Adam (1991) *Democracy and the Market: Political and Economic Reforms in Eastern Europe and Latin America*, New York: Cambridge University Press.

Raimondo, Estelle (2019) "Social contracts matter for development: what can the World Bank do about it?," Independent Evaluation Group, Blog post, November 19, at https://ieg.worldbankgroup.org/blog/social-contracts -matter-development-what-can-world-bank-do-about-it.

Rajan, Raghuram (2019) *The Third Pillar: How Markets and the State Leave the Community Behind*, New York: Penguin.

Rao, Vijayendra (2019) "Process-policy and outcome-policy: rethinking how to address poverty and inequality," *Daedalus* 148(3): 181–90.

Rao, Vijayendra (2022) "Can economics become more reflexive? Exploring the potential of mixed methods," Policy Research Working Paper 9918, Washington, DC: World Bank.

Rao, Vijayendra and Michael Woolcock (2007) "The disciplinary monopoly in development research at the World Bank," *Global Governance* 13(4): 479–84.

Rao, Vijayendra, Kripa Ananthpur, and Kabir Malik (2017) "The anatomy of failure: an ethnography of a randomized trial to deepen democracy in rural India," *World Development* 99(11): 481–97.

Ravallion, Martin (2001) "Growth, inequality and poverty: looking beyond averages," *World Development* 29(11): 1803–15.

Raz, Joseph (1977) "The rule of law and its virtue," *Law Quarterly Review* 93: 195–202.

Reich, David (2018) *Who We Are and How We Got Here: Ancient DNA and the New Science of the Human Past*, New York: Vintage Books.

Reynolds, David (2009) *Summits: Six Meetings that Shaped the Twentieth Century*, New York: Basic Books

Rittel, Horst W. J. and Melvin M. Webber (1973) "Dilemmas in a general theory of planning," *Policy Sciences* 4(2): 155–69.

Rodrik, Dani (1999a) "Where did all the growth go? External shocks, social conflict, and growth collapses," *Journal of Economic Growth* 4(4): 385–412.

Rodrik, Dani (1999b) *The New Global Economy and Developing Countries: Making Openness Work*, London: Overseas Development Council.

Roger, Charles B. (2020) *The Origins of Informality: Why the Legal Foundations of Global Governance Are Shifting, and Why It Matters*, New York: Oxford University Press.

Rogers, Patricia and Michael Woolcock (2023) "Process and implementation evaluation methods," in Anu Rangarajan and Diane Paulsell (eds.) *Oxford Handbook of Social Program Design and Implementation Evaluation*, New York: Oxford University Press.

Romer, Paul (1993) "Idea gaps and object gaps in economic development," *Journal of Monetary Economics* 32(3): 543–73.

Rondinelli, Dennis (1983) *Development Projects as Policy Experiments: An Adaptive Approach to Development Administration*, London: Methuen.

Rosling, Hans (2018) *Factfulness: Ten Reasons We're Wrong About the World – And Why Things Are Better than You Think*, New York: Flatiron Books.

Sage, Caroline, Nicholas Menzies, and Michael Woolcock (2010) "Taking the rules of the game seriously: mainstreaming justice in development," in Stephen Golub (ed.) *Legal Empowerment: Practitioners' Perspectives*, Rome: International Development Law Organization, pp. 19–37.

Saraki, Toyin (2016) "There is good news on gender equality – if you look to the developing world," *The Guardian*, December 16.

Schumacher, E. F. (1973) *Small is Beautiful: Economics as If People Mattered*, New York: Harper and Row.

Schumpeter, Joseph (1983 [1934]) *The Theory of Economic Development: An Inquiry into Profits, Capital, Credit, Interest, and the Business Cycle*, New Brunswick, NJ: Transaction Publishers.

Scott, James C. (1998) *Seeing Like a State: How Certain*

Schemes to Improve the Human Condition Have Failed, New Haven: Yale University Press.

Scott, James C. (2009) *The Art of Not Being Governed: An Anarchist History of Upland Southeast Asia,* New Haven: Yale University Press.

Scott, James C. (2017) *Against the Grain: A Deep History of the Earliest States,* New Haven: Yale University Press.

Seawright, Jason (2016) "The case for selecting cases that are deviant or extreme on the independent variable," *Sociological Methods & Research* 45(3): 493–525.

Sherman, Sandra (2001) *Imagining Poverty: Quantification and the Decline of Paternalism,* Columbus, OH: Ohio University Press.

Siedentop, Larry (2014) *Inventing the Individual: The Origins of Western Liberalism,* Cambridge, MA: Harvard University Press.

Slack, Paul (2015) *The Invention of Improvement: Information and Material Progress in Seventeenth-Century England,* Oxford: Oxford University Press.

Smith, Richard (2011) "Social security as a developmental institution? The relative efficacy of poor relief provisions under the English Old Poor Law," in C. A. Bayly, Vijayendra Rao, Simon Szreter, and Michael Woolcock (eds.) *History, Historians and Development Policy: A Necessary Dialogue,* Manchester: Manchester University Press, pp. 75–102.

Smith, Shannon L., Kelly Blake, Carol R. Olson, and Irene Tessaro (2002) "Community entry in conducting rural focus groups: process, legitimacy, and lessons learned," *The Journal of Rural Health* 18(1): 118–24.

Solar, Peter M. (1995) "Poor relief and English economic development before the industrial revolution," *The Economic History Review* 48(1): 1–22.

Starr, Paul (2019) *Entrenchment: Wealth, Power and the Constitution of Democratic Societies,* New Haven: Yale University Press.

Starr, S. Frederick (2013) *Lost Enlightenment: Central Asia's Golden Age from the Arab Conquest to Tamerlane.* Princeton, NJ: Princeton University Press.

Steil, Benn (2013) *The Battle of Bretton Woods: John Maynard*

Keynes, Harry Dexter White, and the Making of a New World Order, Princeton, NJ: Princeton University Press.

Sterck, Olivier, Max Roser, Mthuli Ncube, and Stefan Thewissen (2018) "Allocation of development assistance for health: is the predominance of national income justified?" *Health Policy and Planning* 33(1): i14–i23.

Stiglitz, Joseph (2007) *Making Globalization Work*, New York: W. W. Norton.

Suddaby, Roy, Alex Bitektine, and Patrick Haack (2017) "Legitimacy," *Academy of Management Annals* 11(1): 451–78.

Sunstein, Cass (1993) *The Partial Constitution*, Cambridge, MA: Harvard University Press.

Swedberg, Richard (1990) *Economics and Sociology: Redefining Their Boundaries – Conversations with Economists and Sociologists*, Princeton, NJ: Princeton University Press.

Szreter, Simon (1997) "Economic growth, disruption, deprivation, disease, and death: on the importance of the politics of public health for development," *Population and Development Review* 23(4): 693–728.

Tai, Don Bambino Geno, Aditya Shah, Chyke A. Doubeni, Irene G. Sia, and Mark L. Wieland (2021) "The disproportionate impact of COVID-19 on racial and ethnic minorities in the United States," *Clinical Infectious Diseases* 72(4): 703–6.

Talbott, Strobe (2009) *The Great Experiment: The Story of Ancient Empires, Modern States and the Quest for a Global Nation*, New York: Simon & Schuster.

Tallberg, Jonas and Michael Zürn (2019) "The legitimacy and legitimation of international organizations: introduction and framework," *The Review of International Organizations* 14(4): 581–606.

Tamanaha, Brian (2004) *On the Rule of Law: History, Politics, Theory*, New York: Cambridge University Press.

Tamanaha, Brian (2011) "The primacy of society and the failures of law and development," *Cornell International Law Journal* 44: 209–47.

Tamanaha, Brian (2021a) "Legal pluralism across the global

South: colonial origins and contemporary consequences," *The Journal of Legal Pluralism and Unofficial Law* 53(2): 168–205.

Tamanaha, Brian (2021b) *Legal Pluralism Explained: Theory, Consequences*, New York: Oxford University Press.

Tamanaha, Brian, Caroline Sage and Michael Woolcock (eds.) (2012) *Legal Pluralism and Development: Scholars and Practitioners in Dialogue*, New York: Cambridge University Press.

Taylor, Charles (1992) *Sources of the Self: The Making of the Modern Identity*, Cambridge, MA: Harvard University Press.

The Economist (2017) "Interracial marriages are rising in America," June 12, at https://www.economist.com /graphic-detail/2017/06/12/interracial-marriages-are-rising -in-america.

The Economist (2019) "The glass ceiling index," March 8, at https://www.economist.com/graphic-detail/2019/03/08 /the-glass-ceiling-index.

Trebilcock, Michael and Ronald Daniels (2008) *Rule of Law Reform and Development: Charting the Fragile Path of Progress*, Cheltenham: Edward Elgar.

Trubek, David and Marc Galanter (1974) "Scholars in self-estrangement: some reflections on the crisis in law and development studies in the United States," *Wisconsin Law Review* 4: 1062–102.

Turner, Mark and David Hulme (1997) *Governance, Administration and Development: Making the State Work*, New York: Palgrave.

Tyler, Tom (2003) "Procedural justice, legitimacy, and the effective rule of law," *Crime and Justice* 30: 283–357.

Tyler, Tom (2006) *Why People Obey the Law*, Princeton, NJ: Princeton University Press.

UNESCO (2019) *Global Education Monitoring Report 2019: Building Bridges for Gender Equality*, Paris: UNESCO.

Uphoff, Norman (1992) *Learning from Gal Oya: Possibilities for Participatory Development and Post-Newtonian Social Science*, Ithaca, NY: Cornell University Press.

van Bavel, Bas and Auke Rijpma (2016) "How important were formalized charity and social spending before the rise of the welfare state? A long-run analysis of selected western European cases, 1400–1850," *The Economic History Review* 69(1): 159–87.

Virilio, Paul (1999) *Politics of the Very Worst*, New York: Semiotext(e).

Wagner, Peter (2016) *Progress: A Reconstruction*, Cambridge: Polity Press.

Waldron, Jeremy (2002) "Is the rule of law an essentially contested concept (in Florida)?" *Law and Philosophy* 21: 137–64.

Wetterberg, Anna, Jon R. Jellema, and Leni Dharmawan (2013) "The local level institutions study three: overview," Washington, DC: World Bank.

Wilkinson, Alissa (2020) "We got comfortable with Hamilton. The new film reminds us how risky it is," *Vox*, July 2, at https://www.vox.com/21308627/hamilton-movie-review -disney-2020.

Williams, Martin (2017) "The political economy of unfinished development projects: corruption, clientelism, or collective choice?" *American Political Science Review* 111(4): 705–22.

Winchester, Simon (2021) *Land: How the Hunger for Ownership Shaped the Modern World*, New York: Harper Collins.

Wong, R. Bin (1997) *China Transformed: Historical Change and the Limits of European Experience*, Ithaca, NY: Cornell University Press.

Wong, Susan and Scott Guggenheim (2018) "Community-driven development: myths and realities," Policy Research Working Paper 8435, Washington, DC: World Bank.

Woolcock, Michael (2007) "Higher education, policy schools, and international development studies: what should Masters degree students be taught?" *Journal of International Development* 19(1): 55–73.

Woolcock, Michael (2009) "Toward a plurality of methods in project evaluation: a contextualized approach to under-standing impact trajectories and efficacy," *Journal of Development Effectiveness* 1(1): 1–14.

Woolcock, Michael (2012) "Dueling development visions: shaping the World Bank for the future," World Bank, Let's Talk Development Blog, April 13, at https://blogs.worldbank.org/developmenttalk/what-exactly-is-development.

Woolcock, Michael (2017) "Social institutions and the development process: using cross-disciplinary insights to build an alternative aid architecture," *Polymath* 7(2): 5–30.

Woolcock, Michael (2019a) "When do development projects enhance community well-being?" *International Journal of Community Well-Being* 2(2): 81–9.

Woolcock, Michael (2019b) "Why does Hirschmanian development remain mired on the margins? Because implementation (and reform) really is 'a long voyage of discovery,'" in Luca Mendolesi and Nicoletta Stame (eds.) *A Bias for Hope: Second Conference on Albert Hirschman's Legacy*, Rome: Italic Digital Editions, pp. 78–95.

Woolcock, Michael (2019c) "Reasons for using mixed methods in the evaluation of complex projects," in Michiru Nagatsu and Attilia Ruzzene (eds.) *Contemporary Philosophy and Social Science: An Interdisciplinary Dialogue*, London: Bloomsbury Academic, pp. 149–71.

Woolcock, Michael (2020) "Assessing and interpreting complex development interventions: three key principles and two (intractable?) conundrums," in Horst Fischer and Anselm Schneider (eds.) *Changing Dimensions of the International Development System: New Realities and Working Differently to Overcome Delivery Challenges*, Zurich: LIT VERLAG GmbH & Co. KGWien, pp. 181–95.

Woolcock, Michael (2022) "What works here? Using case studies to generate 'key facts' about complex development programs," in Jennifer Widner, Michael Woolcock, and Daniel Ortega Nieto (eds.) *The Case for Case Studies: Methods and Applications in International Development*, New York: Cambridge University Press, pp. 87–116.

Woolcock, Michael and Kate Bridges (2019) "The fly on the back of the bird on the back of the elephant: how can you measure whether your adaptive approach is actually fixing problems that matter?" World Bank, Let's Talk Development Blog, November 4, at https://blogs.worldbank.org/developmenttalk/fly-bird-elephant-how-can-you-measure-whether-your-adaptive-approach-actually.

Woolcock, Michael, Simon Szreter, and Vijayendra Rao (2011) "How and why does history matter for development policy?" *Journal of Development Studies* 47(1): 70–96.

World Bank (2005) *World Development Report 2006: Equity and Development*, New York: Oxford University Press.

World Bank (2011) *World Development Report 2011: Conflict, Security and Development*, Washington, DC: World Bank.

World Bank (2015a) "Financial reporting and oversight improvement project: mid term review report," Washington, DC: World Bank Group.

World Bank (2015b) *World Development Report 2015: Mind, Society, and Behavior*, Washington, DC: World Bank.

World Bank (2016) *Making Politics Work for Development*, Washington, DC: World Bank.

World Bank (2017a) *World Development Report 2017: Governance and the Law*, Washington, DC: World Bank.

World Bank (2017b) "Social service delivery in violent contexts: achieving results against the odds – a Report from Afghanistan, Pakistan and Nepal," Washington, DC: World Bank.

World Bank (2018a) "Justice for the Poor reflection note," Mimeo, Washington, DC: World Bank.

World Bank (2018b) *World Development Report 2018: Learning to Realize Education's Promise*, Washington, DC: World Bank.

World Bank (2020a) "The fallout of war: the regional consequences of the conflict in Syria," Washington, DC: World Bank.

World Bank (2020b) *Somalia Urbanization Review: Fostering Cities as Anchors of Development*, Washington, DC: World Bank.

World Bank (2020c) *Global Economic Prospects*, Washington, DC: World Bank.

World Bank (2020d) *Disability Inclusion in Latin America*, Washington, DC: World Bank.

World Bank (2020e) *Poverty and Shared Prosperity Report 2020: Reversals of Fortune*, Washington, DC: World Bank.

World Bank (2021) *World Bank Engagement in Situations of Conflict: An Independent Evaluation*, Washington, DC: World Bank.

Wydick, Bruce, Paul Glewwe, and Laine Rutledge (2013) "Does international child sponsorship work? A six-country study of impacts on adult life outcomes," *Journal of Political Economy* 121(2): 393–436.

Zürn, Michael (2004) "Global governance and legitimacy problems," *Government and Opposition* 39(2): 260–87.

Index